Lifting as we Climb

evette dionne

BLACK WOMEN'S BATTLE FOR THE BALLOT BOX

VIKING

VIKING
An imprint of Penguin Random House LLC, New York

First published in the United States of America by Viking,
an imprint of Penguin Random House LLC, 2020

Visit us online at penguinrandomhouse.com

LIBRARY OF CONGRESS CATALOGING-IN-PUBLICATION DATA IS AVAILABLE
ISBN 9780451481542

Printed in the United States of America

Set in Sabon MT Std   Book design by Kate Renner

10   9   8   7   6   5   4   3   2   1

For every Black woman, past or present,
who has sacrificed their all to give us the vote.

Contents

Not the History You Learned in School

On November 8, 2016, it seemed inevitable that America would finally elect its first woman president. Hillary Rodham Clinton, a former lawyer, first lady, senator, and secretary of state, seemed like a shoo-in for commander in chief. It was the first time that Americans would be able to cast a ballot for a female president on the ticket of a major political party, so many women around the United States were buzzing with excitement. I was one of those women. I was living in New York City at the time, and working as a senior news editor at a website for women. Everywhere, the atmosphere was thick with anticipation; women who didn't know each other smiled as we boarded the subway, passed by each other at voting locations, and thought about the history unrolling in real time. We'd one day be able to tell the young people in our lives—our children, our nieces and nephews, our little cousins—about the day that a woman first became president of the United States. Happiness vibrated through the air, almost as if we could reach out and touch it.

On that second Tuesday in November, thousands of women traveled to Rochester, New York, to visit the grave of the prominent suffragist Susan B. Anthony, who fought for sixty years to help women gain the right to vote. Visitors plastered "I Voted" stickers on her grave. Many of them wore white clothing, the color associated with suffragists, to honor their foremothers who lobbied, marched, and made sacrifices to ensure that women in the United States could vote without any obstacles.

Susan B. Anthony died fourteen years before the Nineteenth Amendment, which granted women the right to vote, was ratified on August 26, 1920. And yet, some women saw Hillary Clinton's presidential run as a reward for all of Anthony's hard work. Clinton embodied Anthony's dream, not only for women to gain the right to vote, but for women to run for office—*and win*. On Election Day 2016, Deborah Hughes, the executive director of the National Susan B. Anthony Museum and House, said that there were more visitors at her grave than ever before. "This is so powerful," Hughes said. "Someone asked me if there's ever been a line this long—there's never been a line." There is no doubt that Anthony deserved all that love. However, there were other suffragists whose contributions to the cause were erased and forgotten; their graves were bare on November 8, 2016. Black women also fought, were beaten or jailed, and faced serious, sometimes violent opposition to gain the right to vote—even after 1920. Where were their stickers?

So after I'd cast my ballot for president, written and edited stories about the ongoing election, and settled in to watch the results, I began tweeting. I urged people to place "I Voted" stickers on the graves of Black suffragists like Sojourner Truth, Frances Ellen Watkins Harper, Nannie Helen Burroughs, Shirley Chisholm, and Fannie Lou Hamer, who have fought for generations, from the end of legal enslavement in the United States to the present day, to help secure voting rights for Black people. Whether it was creating organizations that helped elect Black congresspeople, as Anna Julia Cooper did when she cofounded the Colored Women's League, or running for office, as Chisholm did when she became the first Black woman to be elected to Congress, or encouraging Black people to register to vote during the Civil Rights Movement, as Hamer did, Black women have put themselves in the line of fire over and over again. Yet, when people learn about the long fight for women's suffrage in the United States, it's often an incomplete lesson. Students hear about Susan B. Anthony and Elizabeth Cady Stanton, but not much about Josephine St. Pierre Ruffin or Mary Church Terrell.

To my surprise and delight, several people who follow me on Twitter heeded my suggestion. They traveled to the graves of some of these Black suffragists, put their "I Voted" stickers on the women's tombstones, and sent me pictures and videos through e-mail and direct messages on social-media sites. Though Clinton lost the 2016 election, it was an important moment for generations of women. It was also an important moment that allowed me to shed light on the work that so many Black women have done for centuries to guarantee that all Americans can exercise their right to vote. But unfortunately, this history is still not taught as often as it should be, and many of us don't know about it until we seek out the knowledge on our own as adults.

Once upon a time, I was a precocious child who read a lot of books and asked a lot of questions. Back then, I was often the only Black child in classes led by white teachers, and we would spend months discussing US history. We learned about the thirteen original colonies, protesters tossing tea into Boston Harbor to oppose Britain's tea tax, and the subsequent American Revolutionary War, which resulted in the colonies separating from Great Britain and becoming an independent nation. We read about slavery, abolition, and the Civil War. We heard about great white inventors, including Thomas Edison and Albert Einstein, and sometimes, my teachers even snuck in information about people who fought for women to gain the right to vote. Black American history, however, was rarely, if ever, taught—except, of course, in February. In the twenty-eight days of that month each year, all my teachers—from kindergarten through high school—stumbled over hundreds of years of history, squeezing it all into a truncated timeline that only told the stories of already notable historical figures, like abolitionist Harriet Tubman, inventor George Washington Carver, and Civil Rights Movement activist Martin Luther King Jr. I felt the lack of understanding of my own history; those lessons left me wanting as a child. I wasn't able to fill in all the gaps that those teachers skipped over until I took an African American history course in college.

August 2020 marks the hundredth anniversary of the ratification of the Nineteenth Amendment. More women participated in the effort to win the race for America's president or vice president in the centennial year than in any other presidential election prior. It's more urgent than ever to ensure that young people know the full history of how they got there: the long and hard battle women fought for the right to vote in the United States. It didn't begin with the 1848 Seneca Falls Convention, which is considered the first women's rights convention in the United States; it didn't end in 1920; and for women of color in particular, it wasn't just about voting. This is a book about the myriad issues that Black women had to overcome as they fought to secure voting rights, including lynching, sexual violence, segregation, and being ignored or abandoned by white suffragists. It is a battle that still wages on as some states continue to erect barriers that make it difficult for all Black people and other people of color to exercise their voting rights, including laws that require people to present certain forms of ID and pay off fines before being eligible to register or vote.

The history of suffrage in the United States remains pertinent beyond the centennial milestone. I hope this book serves as an introduction to the overlooked and forgotten Black women who helped permanently reshape America. It celebrates their triumphs, honors their sacrifices, and gives them the stickers and flowers they've long deserved.

ONE

Abolitionist Women Embrace the Fight

Slavery was a big business in America in the early 1830s. About two million of the country's thirteen million residents were enslaved, and the enslaved population—who were considered the property of their owners—was worth hundreds of millions of dollars in modern-day money. So ending enslavement was a wildly unpopular idea in the South and in other parts of the country. Plus, enslaved people did the hard work of planting and harvesting sugarcane, tobacco, cotton, and other crops; they were one of the driving forces of the American economy. Now, more than 150 years after the 1865 ratification of the Thirteenth Amendment, which formally ended slavery in the United States, it might be difficult to understand why there was so much support for enslaving fellow humans and using brutality, including whipping and torturing people, to keep them enslaved. At the time, though, many white Americans—both those who owned people and those who didn't—considered slavery a necessary evil. How else could a new country survive and grow its economy? Congress banned the importation of human cargo into the United States in 1808, but the population of enslaved people in America continued to grow due to "natural increase," enslaved women having an average of between nine and ten children in their lifetimes. Children fathered by plantation owners and born to enslaved women became enslaved. These were among the factors that caused the US slave population to increase between 25 percent and 33 percent every year. Though many people in the United States, including slaveholders, were aware of the brutality of the institution, for slaveholders, the economic benefits far outweighed the moral conundrum that it presented.

After more than two hundred years of slavery as an American way of life, a number of devoutly religious white men, including professor and activist Theodore Dwight Weld, journalist William Lloyd Garrison, businessmen Arthur and Lewis Tappan, and newspaper owner Benjamin Lundy, publicly questioned whether the moral failure of slavery outweighed its perceived economic necessity. "Enslave the liberty of but one human being and the liberties of the world are put in peril," Garrison wrote in his anti-slavery newspaper, the *Liberator*, a quote that illustrated his and other people's approach to abolition or abolishing slavery. These men, many of whom were Quakers, developed a strategic plan: They created anti-slavery organizations and published newspapers, like the *Genius of Emancipation* and the *Liberator*, and delivered speeches and lectures to turn public opinion against slavery, encourage plantation owners to free the people they'd enslaved, and help craft laws that preserved and protected the rights of formerly enslaved people. The anti-slavery movement spread throughout the United States and took hold in eastern cities like Philadelphia, where Black women like Sarah Mapps Douglass also joined the abolition cause.

Frederick Douglass (no relation to Sarah Mapps Douglass), who escaped from a plantation in Baltimore, Maryland, in 1838, became one of the anti-slavery movement's most recognizable and prominent speakers. He published the *North Star*, an abolitionist newspaper, and traveled throughout Northern states, including New York and Pennsylvania, delivering firecracker speeches that called for the end of slavery. "Whether we turn to the declarations of the past, or to the professions of the present, the conduct of the nation seems equally hideous and revolting," he said to a raucous crowd during a Fourth of July celebration in Rochester, New York, in 1852. "America is false

FUGITIVE SLAVE ACTS OF 1793 AND 1850

Vermont abolished slavery in 1777; when it joined the United States in 1791, it was the only state to not have anyone enslaved within its borders. Pennsylvania, New Hampshire, Massachusetts, Connecticut, and Rhode Island abolished slavery between 1780 and 1784. Meanwhile, in the South, there was a reaffirmed commitment to slavery, even as enslaved people began escaping and relocating to Northern states where they were free.

Since enslaved people were legally considered property, Congress, spurred by the personal interests of Southern congressional leaders, passed the Fugitive Slave Act of 1793. This federal law required all states, including free ones, to allow for the capture of escaped slaves and the return to their original owners. The act also declared that all children born to people who were formerly enslaved and escaped were considered the property of that escaped person's original owner—and that they could be returned to the owner at any point in their lives, even if these children had been born after their parent escaped.

In opposition, Northern states either didn't enforce the federal law or passed state laws that guaranteed fugitive slaves the right to a trial. Several states even to the past, false to the present, and solemnly binds herself to be false to the future."

Men, including Douglass, were perceived as the principal leaders of the anti-slavery movement. In the nineteenth century, women were considered the inferior or lesser sex. Though many male abolitionists were progressive about ending slavery, they were less welcoming to the idea that women would leave their domestic duties, such as cooking, cleaning, and child-rearing, and join the public fight to abolish slavery. Despite these sexist attitudes, a number of women

Slave owners often created flyers that promised a reward in exchange for the return of their "property." This is a fugitive slave ad for someone who escaped from Ripley County, Missouri, in 1860.

passed laws that prevented elected officials from helping in the capture and return of fugitives.

In 1850, Southern states began threatening to secede from the United States because enslaved people continued to escape and flee to Northern states that welcomed them and protected them from slave catchers. In order to quell this uprising, Senator Henry Clay of Kentucky encouraged Congress to pass another law that required all states to permit the capture and return of free people to their former plantations. Unlike the Fugitive Slave Act of 1793, this act called for a $1,000 fine and/or six months' imprisonment for anyone who knew about runaway slaves and didn't report them.

became instrumental in spreading abolitionist ideas. Some of these women, such as activists Mary Edmonson, Emily Edmonson, Maria Stewart, and Ellen Craft, delivered speeches that argued for the end of slavery; others, like poet Frances Ellen Watkins Harper and author Mary Prince, made slavery a prominent theme throughout their

SARAH MAPPS DOUGLASS

In addition to being an abolitionist and an educator, Sarah Mapps Douglass was also an accomplished painter. She did this picture of a honeysuckle sometime in 1845.

Sarah Mapps Douglass (1806–1882), a Philadelphia native, lived among the more than two thousand free Black people in that city. Philadelphia was a bustling industrial center with jobs and housing opportunities for people who'd escaped slavery, and protections against slave catchers who wanted to return them to plantations throughout the South.

Douglass had unusual advantages for a Black woman of that time: She'd been born to a prominent and well-educated free family in 1806. Douglass's mother, Grace, was a member of the Quaker faith, a religious tradition whose parishioners believed all people were created equal under God, slavery was immoral, and therefore, it was their Christian duty to end the practice. Sarah's father, Robert, bumped elbows with other influential free Blacks who visited his home and his popular salon where he styled their hair. Her grandfather was one of the early members of the Free African Society, an organization that free Black men in Philadelphia founded in 1787 to help newly escaped Black people find jobs and housing.

Sarah was homeschooled by her parents and then attended a local school that her mother founded to educate Black children. She went off to college in the early 1820s. When she graduated, she first taught in New York City, and then returned to Philadelphia in the early 1830s to begin teaching at a Free African School for writing; still other women leveraged their roles as wives and mothers and turned their abolitionist views into actions, such as boycotting products that were produced from slave labor. These women stopped purchasing cotton, sugar, and tobacco grown in Southern states, and encouraged other women in their communities to do so as well.

Girls, an institution designed specifically to teach Black girls.

The abolition movement was brewing, but Douglass wasn't eager to be a part of it at first. In many ways, she had been insulated from the true horrors of slavery. Any information she gained came secondhand, so she was initially reluctant to get involved: "It is true, the wail of the captive sometimes came to my ear in the midst of my happiness, and caused my heart to bleed for his wrongs; but, alas! the impression was as evanescent as the early cloud and morning dew," Douglass said during a June 1832 speech delivered at the Female Literary Society of Philadelphia.

But then Douglass learned about a revolt in Southampton County, Virginia, in 1831, led by an enslaved man named Nat Turner. Turner and some of his coconspirators were captured and executed. Southern states became even more aggressive and repressive. They tried to force Philadelphia to keep Black people within its city limits and to prevent the city from accepting newly escaped Blacks. The number of slave catchers who tracked fugitives from plantations and returned them to slavery increased. Douglass had an epiphany: She couldn't pretend slavery wasn't a thriving industry below the line that separated Pennsylvania and other free states from the horrors taking place in the South. She realized that freedom was precarious. It could be easily snatched away from her, her family, and the Black people she encountered every day. She had to become more involved in the abolition movement to end slavery or her own freedom would eventually be compromised—and there was nothing more important than being free and helping others gain their freedom.

Sarah Mapps Douglass's values informed her crusade to become an abolitionist. She was one of the only women, especially Black women, to be taken seriously and treated as an equal within the movement.

Sarah Mapps Douglass also put her money where her mouth was: In 1831, she and a number of her prominent Black friends came together to raise money for William Lloyd Garrison's abolitionist newspaper, the *Liberator*, for which she also contributed articles. On September 20, 1831, Douglass and her friends also formed the Female Literary Association, a weekly meeting in Philadelphia for Black women to share their own writings and important readings they'd come across. Each week, twenty members gathered together to "recite and read" anonymous stories written by each of them and then dropped in a box to be taken out and shared. Their overall goals went beyond reading and discussion. Members of the association wanted to use their "endeavors to enlighten the understanding, to cultivate the talents entrusted to our keeping, that by so doing, we may in a great measure, break down the strong barrier of prejudice." For Black woman abolitionists like Douglass, this kind of community gathering helped them learn about big, contemporary issues, including slavery.

Despite their ongoing commitment to ending slavery and Douglass's close friendship with Garrison, there's no doubt that the abolitionist movement had a sexism problem: On December 4, 1833, sixty-four abolitionists from ten states gathered at the Adelphi Building in Philadelphia to create the American Anti-Slavery Society (AASS), an organization that perceived slavery as a "heinous crime in the sight of God." The organization's goal was to immediately end slavery and give Black Americans "civil and religious privileges" equal to those of white people in the United States. However, only white woman abolitionists were invited to the meeting, and they were relegated to the sidelines. Lucretia Mott, Lydia White, Esther Moore, and Sidney Ann Lewis were present, but they weren't asked to participate or sign the AASS's new constitution. They were to be seen and

FRANCES ELLEN WATKINS HARPER

Frances Ellen Watkins Harper (1825–1911) was born to free parents in Baltimore, Maryland, a city that still had enslaved people within its borders. After her parents died, writing became a salvation for Harper. When she wasn't working as a seamstress for white families, Harper crafted poems—about the grief she felt after her parents' deaths, about the discrimination she encountered in Baltimore, and about her hope for a future where all people were free. By the time she was twenty, she'd written enough material to publish *Forest Leaves*, a collection of poetry that marked her as an important voice in the abolition movement. She also later became famous for her novel *Iola Leroy, or Shadows Uplifted* (1892), one of the first books published by a Black woman in the United States.

In 1850, Harper left Baltimore to become the first woman teacher at Union Seminary in Wilberforce, Ohio. Two years later, Harper left Union Seminary to begin teaching in Little York, Pennsylvania, where she worked as part of the Underground Railroad network of safe houses and helped enslaved people as they fled from the South to free states in the North.

Awakened to the horrors of slavery, Harper dedicated herself to the cause of abolition. She joined the American Anti-Slavery Society (AASS) and lectured throughout the Northeast and Canada about the importance of suffrage and the need to end the institution of slavery. "We are all bound up together in one great bundle of humanity, and society cannot trample on the weakest and feeblest of its members without receiving the curse in its own soul," she said during an 1866 speech at the National Woman's Rights Convention in New York. Eventually, Harper became a member of the American Woman Suffrage Association (AWSA), and she spent the latter portion of her life fighting to gain the right to vote for all women. "I claim for the negro protection in every right with which the government has invested him," she said in an 1891 speech at a National Council of Women Convention in Washington, DC. "Whether it was wise or unwise, the government has exchanged the fetters on his wrist for the ballot in his right hand, and men cannot vitiate his vote by fraud, or intimidate the voter by violence, without being untrue to the genius and spirit of our government, and bringing demoralization into their own political life and ranks."

not heard, sent to the back of the room to become spectators instead of active participants in determining the priorities of this newfound organization. In fact, they were so overlooked that the AASS encouraged the women in attendance to create their own anti-slavery organizations.

So, on December 9, 1833, five days after the AASS was formed, Mott gathered a group of women, mostly Quakers, in schoolteacher Catherine McDermott's small classroom to create their own female anti-slavery society. When Sarah Mapps Douglass and her mother learned that an anti-slavery society for women was being formed, there was no way they'd miss a chance to attend. They headed to the school for the inaugural meeting of the Philadelphia Female Anti-Slavery Society (PFASS). Like its male counterpart the AASS, the PFASS's mission was to "elevate the people of color from their present degraded situation to the full enjoyment of their rights and to increased usefulness in society." When Douglass and her mother arrived in the cramped classroom, they were greeted by a number of other female abolitionists, both white and Black. It was an unusual situation; typically, white and Black women were segregated, relegated to their own society and communities. They generally didn't attend the same schools or churches, and most of the time, they weren't even buried in the same graveyards, but from the beginning, Black women were integral members of the PFASS.

Lucretia Mott (1793–1880) was born and raised in Nantucket, Massachusetts. Her Quaker parents instilled in her the idea that women and men had equal abilities and worth. She attended the Nine Partners Boarding School, where she became known as a small but mighty "spitfire" who spoke her mind. As an adult, Mott became an active and vocal abolitionist because of her strong religious beliefs. She often faced criticism from men who believed that women should have a diminished role in the movement, so she joined forces with other women, including Sarah Mapps Douglass, to form the PFASS.

At that first meeting, Sarah Mapps Douglass and her mother greeted and exchanged pleasantries with a number of other Black women, including Margaretta Forten, who along with her daughters, Sarah and Harriet, was part of a prominent free Black family that included James Forten, one of the organizers of the AASS, and Hetty Reckless, who had escaped from a plantation in New Jersey in 1826 and begun operating a part of the

The Philadelphia Female Anti-Slavery Society was founded by woman abolitionists, both white and Black, who were sidelined within the male-dominated American Anti-Slavery Society.

Underground Railroad. These women weren't treated as inferiors or made to feel as if their opinions didn't matter because they were Black. Instead, they helped draft the PFASS's constitution and priorities. A committee of fourteen women—both white and Black—drafted a constitution that declared that slavery was "contrary to the laws of God." The PFASS also created a governing body that included a president, corresponding secretary, treasurer, librarian, and recording secretary; set up monthly meetings; and began spreading the word that the PFASS was open to all—not just white women, but *all* women.

Abolition wasn't an abstract concept for Black women in the 1840s. A great number of them were still enslaved or had fled by foot to free states where, at any moment, they could be captured and returned to slavery. For them, ending slavery wasn't just about being on the right side of history or taking a moral stance. For Black women, abolition meant the difference between living freely and without fear and being sent back to plantations where they would surely be tortured for escaping and their children could be sold away from them at any time. Many of these women were active abolitionists because they had a firsthand understanding of how high the stakes were for themselves and their families.

Abolition, in the PFASS's view, was everyone's work. But Black women were an essential part of the movement because

THE FORTEN FAMILY

Harriet, Sarah Louisa, Margaretta, and Charlotte Forten were powerhouses. These free Black women were members of a wealthy, prominent family in Philadelphia, Pennsylvania, that was committed to abolition. They worked with the Philadelphia Female Anti-Slavery Society to send petitions to the Pennsylvania state legislature to encourage them to abolish slavery. Their individual and collective efforts helped raise awareness about abolition in Philadelphia and throughout the North.

Each of the Forten women was formidable in her own right. Margaretta (1806–1875) toured the country throughout the 1840s, delivering speeches about ending slavery and granting women suffrage; she eventually opened her own school in Philadelphia for Black children. Sarah Louisa (1814–1883) wrote poetry about abolition for the *Liberator*, sometimes using a pen name. Harriet (1810–1875) and her husband, Robert Purvis, turned their home on Ninth and Lombard Street in Philadelphia into a station for the Underground Railroad. When Charlotte Forten Grimké (1837–1914) began attending school in Salem, Massachusetts, in 1854, she started chronicling her day-to-day life in a journal. That journal was published in its entirety long after her death and is considered one of the earliest writings from a free Black woman to explore life in the nineteenth and twentieth centuries.

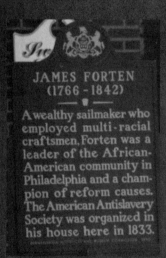

JAMES FORTEN
(1766 - 1842)

A wealthy sailmaker who employed multi-racial craftsmen, Forten was a leader of the African-American community in Philadelphia and a champion of reform causes. The American Antislavery Society was organized in his house here in 1833.

they—especially the abolitionists who were formerly enslaved—understood, far too well, the impact of slavery. They could and did spread the word about the true nature of this terrible institution through pamphlets, books, and speeches far more effectively than those who'd never directly experienced living in slavery. Fearless women, like Hetty Reckless and Harriet Jacobs, unflinchingly told their stories. So did other free Black women who weren't a part of

HETTY RECKLESS

Hetty Reckless (1776–1881), who was born on a plantation in Salem, New Jersey, was vital to the work of the PFASS. She was originally owned by Jane Gibson Johnson, one of the wealthiest women in Salem; when Jane died, ownership of the enslaved woman was transferred to Jane's son, Colonel Robert Gibbon Johnson. Hetty was moved to Johnson Hall, an extraordinarily elaborate home with enough space for Robert, his wife, and the people he enslaved. It was there that Reckless encountered unending brutality from Robert's second wife, Juliana Zantzinger, including having her front teeth knocked out and having strands of her hair mercilessly ripped from her skull.

The punishments were so severe that Reckless fled the plantation in 1826 in the middle of the night with her daughter in tow. She convincingly lied about being emancipated by her previous owner and boarded a stagecoach that took the fleeing mother and child from Salem to Philadelphia. In the years between her flight and her arrival in that classroom on December 9 for the first PFASS meeting, Reckless had fought with the Johnsons, trying to prevent herself and her daughter from being returned to that Salem plantation where she'd been violated time and again. Reckless, who understood fully what was at risk, became an integral part of the Underground Railroad and managed one of its safe houses on Rodman Street in Philadelphia; she devoted much of her time to helping end slavery.

HARRIET JACOBS

Harriet Jacobs (1813–1897) was born enslaved on a plantation in Edenton, North Carolina. From birth, she'd been fighting an uphill battle: Her mother, Delilah, and her father, Daniel, both died when she was a child, so she'd been raised by her mother's owner, Margaret Horniblow. Unlike other enslaved children, who were typically sent to work in fields and pick cotton by the age of five, Jacobs was treated with an unusual kindness. She lived in the house with Horniblow, who taught her how to read, write, and sew. "[We] lived together in a comfortable home, and, though we were all slaves, I was so fondly shielded that I never dreamed that I was a piece of merchandise," she later wrote in her 1861 autobiography *Incidents in the Life of a Slave Girl*. Unfortunately, Jacobs's life drastically changed in 1825 when Horniblow died and she became the property of Dr. James Norcom.

When Jacobs turned fifteen, Norcom began physically abusing her, pressuring her into having a sexual relationship with him, and whispering "foul words" in her ears. Norcom's wife built a cottage for Jacobs more than four miles away from the plantation when she learned how badly her husband was treating the girl. The distance didn't end the harassment; it only escalated. Norcom threatened to sell Jacobs to another plantation if she didn't agree to his increasing sexual demands.

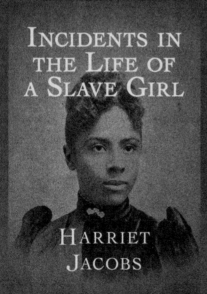

So Jacobs decided to take matters into her own hands.

She started a relationship with one of her neighbors, Samuel Tredwell Sawyer, a white lawyer, and had two children, Joseph and Louisa, with him. It was a "deliberate calculation" to have children with a man "who has no control over you." Jacobs hoped that having children with Sawyer would protect her from Norcom because he'd either feel obligated to free her or Sawyer would buy her freedom. Neither of those things happened, and Norcom's abuse only increased.

Jacobs decided to escape, not only for herself but also for her children. "Whatever slavery might do to me, it could not shackle my children," she later wrote. "If I fell a sacrifice, my little ones were saved."

In June 1835, Harriet Jacobs fled the plantation alone in the dead of night. She was headed for her grandmother and uncle's house. (They had already been freed and wanted to help their kin.) Jacobs hid in a tiny crawlspace above a porch at their house. The crawlspace was only nine feet long and seven feet wide, smaller than a tree house. It was infested with mice and rats that ran over her body. She couldn't move around much in the small space and there weren't any windows or vents, so she rarely got fresh air. Harriet lived like that for seven long years, only coming outside at night to stretch her legs so they wouldn't cramp.

$100 REWARD

WILL be given for the apprehension and delivery of my Servant Girl HARRIET. She is a light mulatto, 21 years of age, about 5 feet 4 inches high, of a thick and corpulent habit, having on her head a thick covering of black hair that curls naturally, but which can be easily combed straight. She speaks easily and fluently, and has an agreeable carriage and address. Being a good seamstress, she has been accustomed to dress well, has a variety of very fine clothes, made in the prevailing fashion, and will probably appear, if abroad, tricked out in gay and fashionable finery. As this girl absconded from the plantation of my son without any known cause or provocation, it is probable she designs to transport herself to the North.

The above reward, with all reasonable charges, will be given for apprehending her, or securing her in any prison or jail within the U. States.

All persons are hereby forewarned against harboring or entertaining her, or being in any way instrumental in her escape, under the most rigorous penalties of the law.
JAMES NORCOM.
Edenton, N. C. June 30

James Norcom's newspaper ad from July 1835.

Jacobs's daunting, unconventional plan worked: Once she'd escaped, Norcom allowed Sawyer to purchase their children's freedom, though Norcom simultaneously circulated posters and newspaper ads that offered a hundred-dollar reward for the recapture of Harriet. In June 1842, more than seven years after she'd initially escaped, Jacobs managed to board a boat in the middle of the night. She paid a handsome sum, most likely given to her by her grandmother and her uncle, to the boat's captain, who smuggled her to the North. When she arrived in Philadelphia, she finally reunited with the children whom she'd risked everything to protect. (Sawyer had been elected to the US House of Representatives, so he brought their children to Philadelphia without actually emancipating them.)

In July 1842, Jacobs moved on to Rochester, New York, where she met noted abolitionist Frederick Douglass. Douglass took a liking to Harriet because she, like him, had escaped slavery. Jacobs went to work at the *North Star*, the abolitionist newspaper that Douglass published. He also helped protect her from slave catchers and Norcom, who still sought her capture. Harriet Jacobs realized that outlawing slavery was the only way she could guarantee that she and her children would remain free. It was a battle that she intended to fight until the day she died or slavery was abolished.

the PFASS but were on the abolition circuit, writing articles, traveling across the North to deliver speeches, and publicly declaring that their cause was critical to the abolition movement.

Sojourner Truth, a formerly enslaved woman born on a plantation in Ulster County, New York, in 1797, and Harriet Tubman, an escaped slave who then traveled to rescue more than three hundred enslaved people from her former plantation, were two of the most famous Black woman abolitionists of that time. Both women understood how brutal and dangerous the institution of slavery was, especially for women and children. Enslaved women occupied unique places on plantations. They were forced to work in planting fields, picking cotton or tobacco, and in plantation homes,

cleaning their master's house, raising their master's children while still caring for their own children, who could be sold to another plantation at any moment. Enslaved women were also in danger of being assaulted by white and Black men alike. What they endured gave them a powerful perspective about both abolition and women's suffrage.

The harrowing stories of enslaved women should have been the linchpin of the American Anti-Slavery Society and Philadelphia Female Anti-Slavery Society's ongoing campaign to persuade the federal government to pass an anti-slavery amendment. Instead, Black woman abolitionists were often overlooked or their voices went unheard.

Black women of the time, including those involved in the PFASS,

began strategizing about how to take their cause and experiences to wider audiences. Educating Black children about abolition was one of Sarah Mapps Douglass's greatest passions, and it was one that the newly formed PFASS strongly supported. Each month, the organization's members, which still numbered less than thirty, met in Clarkson Hall, a building specifically bought to house meetings for abolitionist groups. They discussed how they'd spread "correct information" about the inhumane conditions enslaved people faced every day and how to remove "this foul stain" from America's soil. The devoted members of the PFASS continued their efforts to avoid purchasing

Harriet Tubman (Unknown–1913), on the far left holding a pan, helped all these people escape slavery. Tubman herself had escaped from a plantation in Maryland on September 17, 1849. When she arrived in Philadelphia, she got a job cleaning houses. She learned that two of her children, James and Araminta, were going to be sold, so she retraced her steps to Maryland and retrieved them. From 1849 until 1859, Tubman made several trips back to that plantation and rescued around three hundred enslaved people, including her own parents. She became friends with abolitionists and suffragists, such as Lucretia Mott and Frederick Douglass. By the time the Civil War erupted, Tubman was already deeply—and dangerously—committed to the practice of ending slavery, rescue by rescue.

and using products procured by slave labor. They subscribed to anti-slavery pamphlets, journals, and newspapers; read, discussed, and circulated influential abolitionist Lydia Maria Child's groundbreaking 1833 book, *An Appeal in Favor of That Class of Americans Called Africans*; and most importantly, they collected enough donations to help Sarah Mapps Douglass found a school for Black children in Philadelphia.

While members of the PFASS mobilized, building the organization's foundation and donating enough money to keep it afloat, other

SOJOURNER TRUTH

When Sojourner Truth (1797–1883) was thirteen, she was sold to John Dumont, a brutal slave master in Esopus, New York. Dumont subjected the girl to mental, emotional, and physical violence because she spoke Dutch instead of English. In 1799, New York passed the Gradual Emancipation Act, which required slave owners to free children born into slavery when they became young adults, and said that slaves born before 1799 had to be released by 1827. That's when Truth and Dumont came to an agreement: He would free her before July 4, 1827, "if she would do well and be faithful." However, when that time came, Dumont reneged on his promise and blamed Truth's hand injury, which made her work more slowly. That's when Truth decided to escape with her baby daughter, Sophia, after she spun one hundred pounds of wool. "I did not run off, for I thought that wicked, but I walked off, believing that to be all right," she later explained.

Truth walked and walked and walked until she arrived in New Paltz, New York. She and her daughter arrived on the doorstep of Isaac and Maria Van Wagenen, who took them in, but didn't consider them property. When Dumont located Truth at the Van Wagenens' house and came to retrieve her, the Van Wagenens paid him twenty dollars to keep Truth and her daughter, which he agreed to. She later took Dumont to court for illegally selling her son, Peter, to a plantation owner in Alabama. When she won the case in 1828, she became the first Black woman to successfully sue a white man in the United States.

In 1843, religious convictions convinced her to change her name from Isabella Baumfree to Sojourner Truth because, as she explained, "The Lord gave me [the

Black women who were not members of any official anti-slavery organization were also spreading the gospel of abolition.

Black women like Maria Stewart, who had moved into the middle class only to find that this did not guarantee security, began to look at the connections between abolition and other civil rights. Stewart didn't hesitate when she came across a January 1831 advertisement from William Lloyd Garrison requesting more Black women to contribute stories to his newspaper, the *Liberator*. This was the perfect outlet for Stewart to discuss a number of issues

I SELL THE SHADOW TO SUPPORT THE SUBSTANCE.
SOJOURNER TRUTH.

name] Sojourner because I was to travel up and down the land showing the people their sins and being a sign unto them. Afterward, I told the Lord I wanted another name because everybody else had two names; and the Lord gave me Truth, because I was to declare the truth to the people."

Truth began traveling, preaching the word of God and calling for the end of slavery. She was formally introduced to abolition and suffrage movements in 1844 when she joined the Northampton Association of Education and Industry, a commune of social reformers in Massachusetts. There she met leading abolitionists such as William Lloyd Garrison and Frederick Douglass.

To help fund her activist efforts, Sojourner Truth had photographic cards like the one above made, shot in Detroit in 1864, which includes her famous quote: "I sell the shadow to support the substance." By selling these cards of her image (the "shadow"), she raised money for her real-life causes.

that were now on her doorstep. She was the first person to respond to Garrison's request, and by summer, she'd published a controversial twelve-page pamphlet, "Religion and the Pure Principles of Morality: The Sure Foundation on Which We Must Build." It was a departure from the quiet personae typically associated with Stewart and other women of her class. Stewart's fiery pamphlet caught many people in her community off guard, but it was a freeing moment for her. She finally had a place to express her opinion without being persecuted, and though public speaking was solely the domain of men at that time—women were prohibited or discouraged from giving speeches to mixed audiences of women and men—Stewart had been bottled up for long enough. She was ready to bring her message to the world—or at least her corner of the world—as she proclaimed, "All of the nations of the earth are crying out for Liberty and Equality. Away, away with tyranny and oppression!"

By April 1832, Stewart had turned "Religion and the Pure Principles of Morality" into a speech that she first delivered to a very attentive room at the African American Female Intelligence Society, an organization created by fellow free Black women in Boston. Members listened closely as Stewart stirred them to action, encouraging these women to leave the domain of their homes and enter the realm of abolition: "O, ye daughters of Africa! What have ye done to immortalize your names beyond the grave? What examples have ye set before the rising generation?" Stewart continued delivering variations of this speech to other Black women and even to men, a groundbreaking action that set her apart from other speakers of the time. But by 1833, she'd decided that public speaking was no longer her passion, especially as more and more people began protesting her talks. Her speeches riled up too many people and were considered too radical.

As Stewart wound down her public-speaking career, other Black woman abolitionists were just getting started. From 1833 to 1837, members of the PFASS focused on spreading the mission of abolition throughout the North, and a number of other female anti-slavery organizations also sprang up. There were now anti-slavery organizations

MARIA STEWART

Maria Stewart (1803–1879) of Hartford, Connecticut, was wholly uninterested in being tied to or representing a single anti-slavery organization. It reminded her too much of her troubled and turbulent past: After being orphaned at the age of five, she'd been forced to become a minister's indentured servant. The girl spent her days keeping house—cooking and cleaning—instead of going to school. When Stewart was released from the minister's home at the age of twenty, her priorities were simple: She wanted to find a husband.

In the 1800s, marriage provided a level of financial stability to free Black women like Maria who didn't come from elite or wealthy families and weren't formally educated. In 1826, she met and wed James W. Stewart, a shipping agent who had served in the United States military and received a monthly pension. The marriage meant Maria Stewart could worry less about how she'd get her next meal and more about who she wanted to be. For three years, Stewart simply fulfilled what were perceived as wifely duties: She cooked, cleaned, maintained their home, and participated in the socials put on by other women who were a part of Boston's free middle class. She attended teas, ironed her husband's shirts, and got dressed up when they needed to attend neighborhood events. It was a mundane, humdrum life, but it was hers until James died in 1829 and her entire world was turned upside down. Stewart was left penniless since the executors of her husband's estate refused to grant her his military pension or his inheritance. That act alone pushed her to begin thinking deeply about women's rights, Black people's rights, and how she could draw awareness to her personal plight as well as to these larger issues that impacted so many others.

in New York City, Boston, and Rhode Island; members of each were trying to sway public opinion, but it was difficult to do so without a larger organization that would govern all the anti-slavery societies, bring them together, and share resources.

On August 4, 1836, Maria Weston Chapman, an abolitionist who worked closely alongside Garrison and helped run the Boston Female Anti-Slavery Society, sent a letter to Mary Grew, the PFASS's corresponding secretary. She asked about forming a general executive committee that would help all the female anti-slavery societies develop a singular focus. Grew replied to the letter, saying that having an executive committee was "expedient and desirable" and that each female anti-slavery society should send delegates to New York City in May 1837 for a convention.

As soon as it was decided that there would be a convention of female anti-slavery societies in New York, Sarah Grimké, the abolitionist daughter of a former slave owner in Charleston, South Carolina, sent letters to both the Boston and Philadelphia Female Anti-Slavery Societies to encourage them to send Black woman delegates. Grimké believed that it wasn't possible for the convention to create resolutions that would apply to Black women if they weren't present. Though the PFASS had a number of Black woman members and leaders, including noted abolitionists Sarah McCrummell, the Forten family, and the Douglass family, only 10 percent of the members in all anti-slavery organizations, including female anti-slavery societies, were Black and many didn't have the financial means to travel to New York. Ultimately, only five Black women attended the inaugural convention.

On May 9, 1837, seventy-one woman delegates from ten states

and twenty anti-slavery societies descended on New York City for the inaugural Anti-Slavery Convention of American Women. It was an unprecedented national convention of women in the United States. Woman abolitionists, who believed it was "the duty of every human being to labor to preserve, and to restore to all who are deprived of it, God's gift of freedom," were convening to strategize about how best to approach their crusade.

The convention was successful: The woman abolitionists selected officers for the organization. They adopted resolutions about their roles in the anti-slavery cause and outlined their commitment to immediately abolishing slavery. They declared it "the duty of woman, and the province of woman, to plead her cause of the oppressed in our land and to do all that she can by her voice, and her pen, and her purse, and the influence of her example, to overthrow the horrible system of American slavery." They organized committees that created documents such as an address to free Black people, communications to other female anti-slavery societies that weren't present, and appeals to all American women.

When these women returned from the convention to their respective states after three days, their abolitionist fervor was heightened. Female anti-slavery organizations in a number of different states began bombarding Congress with petitions, asking congressmen to pass legislation that would abolish slavery. Though their efforts weren't successful and slavery continued to be the law of the land, the national conference and the actions that followed marked a turn for woman abolitionists: They realized that in order to achieve their goals, they needed to move away from treating slavery as a moral conundrum. They needed to make slavery a political issue, and in order to do that, they needed to be involved in the political process. Women needed to be equal members of organizations. They needed be able to vote, to run for office, and to be elected—all elements of public life that had long been denied to American women, including and especially Black women.

TWO

"Ain't I a Woman?"
The Cult of True Womanhood

Despite the wisdom that Harriet Jacobs, Frances Ellen Watkins Harper, Maria Stewart, and so many other Black abolitionists provided, their opinions were often cast aside by the very anti-slavery societies in America that initially welcomed them in.

It was more of the same when the British and Foreign Anti-Slavery Society (BFASS) decided to organize a convention in London in 1840 that would bring abolitionists from around the world together. Sarah Mapps Douglass, Margaretta Forten, and Charlotte Forten Grimké were still active members of the PFASS. They could have been invited to London as delegates for the American Anti-Slavery Society. Although there were one hundred female anti-slavery societies in the United States by this time, some founding members of the AASS were staunchly opposed to bringing woman abolitionists to London. One of them, wealthy New York–based abolitionist Lewis Tappan, even went as far as to say, "To put a woman on the committee with men is contrary to the usages of civilized society."

An editor of an abolitionist newspaper in Pittsburgh, Pennsylvania, echoed Tappan's sentiment, writing that Lucretia Mott, the Quaker anti-slavery activist and cofounder of the PFASS, shouldn't travel to London: "We should not be surprised if she should so far forget the true dignity of womanhood in her intractable zeal for what she terms 'principle,' as to attempt to take her seat as a delegate in the 'World's Anti-Slavery Convention.' If she does, and mutual distrust, heart-burnings, and confusion result from such a step, upon her and her advisors will rest the tremendous onus of putting back the day of the slave's redemption."

So, though Black and white female abolitionists staged protests and boycotts, Black women were not invited to the World Anti-Slavery Convention and white women were very reluctantly included. While part of that can be attributed to the racism that ran rampant in some anti-slavery societies, the decision not to attend also came from the delicate social expectations that Black woman abolitionists had to navigate.

At the time, "proper" Black women who'd escaped slavery or had been born free were expected to be four things: religious, pure, domesticated, and submissive. That meant that "true women" would "never lose sight of their familial responsibilities: housekeeping, childbearing, and childrearing." Even when Black women like Sarah Mapps Douglass and Charlotte Forten Grimké attended PFASS meetings, they were expected to display "ladylike" behavior: never be too loud, too bold, too aggressive, or too angry. These were also the lessons that Black girls were learning in schools, including the African Free School, one of the first public schools created for Black students in the late 1700s. Black abolitionist Charles B. Ray took it a step further in 1837 when he wrote in the *Colored American*, a weekly African American newspaper, that "daughters are destined to be wives and mothers—they should, therefore, be taught to know how to manage a house, and govern and instruct children. Without this knowledge, they would be lost, and as mothers distracted, their homes would be in disorder, and their children would grow up loose and without character." This attitude about the role of Black women seeped into the abolition movement, so nobody objected to Black women not being chosen as American delegates or even being invited to travel to London to witness the conference.

Seven white women were selected as delegates of the United States, but when they and other women arrived at London's "densely crowded" Freemasons' Hall, they were forbidden from being seated on the main floor with male abolitionists. Instead, the woman delegates were ushered up to a spectators' gallery. They were forced to sit in a curtained area; they couldn't actually see or participate in the debate—but they could hear male delegates heatedly arguing about whether woman delegates should be allowed onto the convention floor. When male delegates staged a vote, they overwhelmingly decided to exclude women from the convention. For the remainder of the nine days, women would simply be attendees, not delegates actively deciding the future of the global abolition movement. Still, the World Anti-Slavery Convention served an ultimately important purpose: It brought together a number of women, including Lucretia Mott and young activist Elizabeth Cady Stanton, who would later become leaders of the American suffrage movement. Being excluded had lit a fire in these two women. When they returned to the United States, they vowed to "form a society to advocate for the rights of women." It would take more than eight years for that women's rights convention to come together.

In the meantime, abolition remained a focus for many Black women. They continued fighting for abolition while also trying to balance the pressure of working, raising their families, keeping their husbands happy, and being perceived as "respectable" by their community members. Newspapers, churches, and schools were suggesting that women should only focus on "respectable" forms of public life, like going to church, taking their children to school, and hosting parties for their neighbors—not orchestrating petitions to the federal government. Many Black women took this message to heart. Abolition was important, of course, and still at the top of many of their minds, but raising well-educated Black children mattered most. Sarah Mapps Douglass, a founding member of the PFASS, was leading a school for Black girls in Philadelphia and also training other public-school teachers in the area. More than forty students "from our best families, where their morals and manners are equally subjects of care, and deep interest" enrolled in her school, where she taught both practical skills, like cooking and sewing, and more abstract subjects, like science and geometry. Activism still appealed to Douglass, but not enough for her to leave her school for something that many would definitely not consider respectable: a conference for women.

On July 19, 1848, about three hundred people flocked to the Wesleyan Chapel in Seneca Falls, New York, for the first women's rights conference in the United States. Roughly forty men attended. At the outset, Elizabeth Cady Stanton made the convention's purpose clear: "We are assembled to protest against a form of government, existing without the consent of the governed—to declare our right to be free as man is free, to be

Where the American suffrage movement began to take shape.

WOMAN'S RIGHTS CONVENTION.—This convention assembled at Seneca Falls, on the 19th inst. The meeting on the first day was only accessible to females, who drew up and signed a "Declaration of Sentiments," which reads as follows:—When in the course of human events it becomes necessary for one portion of the family of man to assume among the people of earth a position different from that which they have hitherto occupied, but one to which the laws of nature and nature's God entitle them, a decent respect to the opinions of mankind requires that they should declare the causes that impel them to such a course.

We hold these truths to be self-evident—that all men and women are created equal—that they are endowed by their Creator with certain inalienable rights—that among these are life, liberty, and the pursuit of happiness—that to secure these rights governments are instituted, deriving their just powers from the consent of the governed. Whenever any form of government becomes destructive of these ends, it is the right of those who suffer from it to refuse allegiance to it, and to insist upon the institution of a new government, laying its foundation on such principles, and organizing its powers in such form, as to them shall seem most likely to effect their safety and happiness. Prudence, indeed, will dictate that governments long established, should not be changed for light and transient causes, and accordingly all experience hath shown that mankind are more disposed to suffer while evils are sufferable, than to right themselves by abolishing the forms to which they are accustomed; but when a long train of abuses and usurpations, pursuing invariably the same object, evinces a design to reduce them under absolute despotism, it is their right, it is their duty, to throw off such government, and to provide new guards for their future security. Such has been the patient sufferance of the women under this government, and such is now the necessity which constrains them to demand the equal station to which they are entitled.

The history of mankind is a history of repeated injuries and usurpations on the part of man toward woman, having in direct object the establishment of an absolute tyranny over her. To prove this, let facts be submitted to a candid world.

represented in the government which we are taxed to support, to have such disgraceful laws as give man the power to chastise and imprison his wife, to take the wages which she earns, the property which she inherits, and, in case of separation, the children of her love . . . if possible, forever erased from our statute-books." Stanton, Lucretia Mott, and the convention's other organizers were committed to their cause, even as they knew that they were facing an uphill battle, but somehow, women of color were excluded from the Seneca Falls Convention. No Black woman abolitionists attended the convention, most likely because they couldn't afford to travel to Seneca Falls to participate.

Frederick Douglass, who spoke on behalf of the American Anti-Slavery Society, was the only Black person who attended the Seneca Falls gathering. Though Black women and their specific needs weren't considered or represented during the convention, its organizers still proposed the Declaration of Sentiments, a document similar to the Declaration of Independence, which declared that "all men and women are created equal," and that women should have unalienable rights to life, liberty, and the pursuit of happiness. It made sixteen specific claims related to suffrage, property rights, and divorce that were treated as a guiding force for how men in their communities should consider and treat women. The Declaration of Sentiments included a ninth and controversial resolution, added by Elizabeth Cady Stanton in the twilight before the convention ended: "That it is the duty of women of this country to secure to themselves their sacred right to the elective franchise." No woman in the United States had the right to vote, so it was revolutionary for Stanton to include this demand in a founding document. When sixty-eight women and thirty-two men signed the Declaration of

Sixty-eight women and thirty-two men signed the Declaration of Sentiments.

Sentiments, there still wasn't consensus around the ninth resolution, much to Stanton's disappointment. It was the one resolution that didn't gain unanimous support, though Frederick Douglass threw his weight behind it. "I have never yet been able to find one consideration, one argument, or suggestion in favor of man's right to participate in civil government which did not equally apply to the right of woman," he said. Still, Stanton, Mott, and other organizers were prepared for backlash as news of the declaration and the suffrage resolution circulated through the press, rippling far beyond Seneca Falls.

What did those declarations mean for Black women, many of whom were still enslaved? Douglass couldn't give voice to their specific and unique needs, though he wrote in an issue of the *North Star* published shortly after the convention:

> In respect to political rights, we hold woman to be justly entitled to all we claim for man. We go farther, and express our conviction that all political rights which it is expedient for man to exercise, it is equally so for women. All that distinguishes man as an intelligent and accountable being, is equally true of woman; and if that government is only just which governs by the free consent of the governed, there can be no reason in the world for denying to woman the exercise of the elective franchise, or a hand in making and administering the laws of the land. Our doctrine is, that "Right is of no sex."

Mary Ann Shadd Cary, a twenty-five-year-old Black teacher living in Pennsylvania, felt shorted by the Seneca Falls Convention. How could a convention for women not include Black women? In 1848, she wrote a long letter to the *North Star* about the abolition movement's failure to include the voices of Black women. "We should do more and talk less," she wrote in her lengthy letter, which Douglass published in its entirety. "We have been holding conventions for years—we have been assembling together and whining over our difficulties and afflictions, passing resolutions on resolutions to any extent. But it does really seem that we have made but little progress considering our resolves." Cary's letter echoed the sentiments of other Black woman abolitionists who were asking one simple question: Where were Black women's needs positioned within the Declaration of Sentiments?

This question was at the forefront of Sojourner Truth's mind when, two years after the Seneca Falls Convention, Elizabeth Cady Stanton and Lucretia Mott approached William Lloyd Garrison to ask him about Truth both attending and speaking at the National Woman's Rights Convention that Stanton, Mott, and abolitionist Lucy Stone were organizing in Worcester, Massachusetts. Plans for this women's convention had been decided in May 1850 at a special meeting convened during the annual New England Anti-Slavery Society (NEASS) convention, held in Boston, Massachusetts's Melodeon Hall. Garrison, who fought tooth and nail to include women in the American Anti-Slavery Society, supported the creation of a woman's rights convention: "I conceive that the first

Mary Ann Shadd Cary (1823–1893) was born free in Wilmington, Delaware, in October 1823. In 1850, she and her brother moved to Windsor, Ontario, where she started the Provincial Freeman, a weekly newspaper for African Americans who also wanted to immigrate to Canada. Being outside the United States was safer for Cary than being at risk of being thrown into slavery by unscrupulous bounty hunters, though she'd never been enslaved.

thing to be done by the women of this country is to demand their political enfranchisement. Among the 'self-evident truths' announced in the Declaration of Independence is this—'All government derives its just power from the consent of the governed.'"

When the AASS voted overwhelmingly to approve the National Woman's Rights Convention and allow it to take place in October 1850, organizers were overjoyed. The convention was an opportunity to garner more support and "to secure for [woman] political, legal, and social equality with man, until her proper sphere is determined, by what alone should determine it, her Powers and Capacities, strengthened and refined by an education in accordance with her nature."

Sojourner Truth was an important part of this mission for the convention's organizers. More than one thousand delegates from eleven states crowded Worcester's Brinley Hall to hear from a number of different speakers, including Truth, who spoke on both days of the convention about the "trampled women of the plantation." Truth's speech captivated listeners, thanks mostly to her rare gift of being able to "bear down a whole audience with a few simple words." The Worcester convention reached a large number of people, both the men and women who attended and those who learned about it secondhand through newspapers. Coverage was not always favorable. There was also a lot of scorn directed toward these women who dared to suggest that "a woman was just as well qualified to be president as a man." Newspapers mocked the convention, making it seem as if these women's demands were unreasonable. The *New York Herald* even published a satirical article, claiming that the organizers wanted to "abolish the Bible," "abolish the constitution and the laws of the land," and "reorganize society upon a social platform of

SOJOURNER TRUTH.

In the late 1840s, Sojourner Truth began dictating her memoir to her friend Olive Gilbert. When the book, Narrative of Sojourner Truth: A Northern Slave, Emancipated from Bodily Servitude in the State of New York, in 1828, was released in 1850, Truth sold copies at her speeches, which helped her earn a living. Several subsequent editions of the popular book were published. The book is still in print, more than 165 years since its first release.

perfect equality in all things, of sexes and colors." None of this stopped woman organizers.

Every year from 1850 to 1860, a National Woman's Rights Convention was held in a different city, including Philadelphia, Pennsylvania; Syracuse, New York; Cleveland, Ohio; and Cincinnati, Ohio. But as each year passed, fewer and fewer Black women attended. Abolition had to become their priority.

The passage of the Fugitive Slave Act of 1850 had sent many Black abolitionists into a tailspin. Knowing that the federal government could swoop in at any time and return free Black people to the plantations from which they'd escaped (and sometimes sweep up those born free as well) moved many Black people from the sidelines to the center of the anti-slavery fight. Once again, abolition wasn't an abstract concept. It could dictate the outcome of their lives.

As Sojourner Truth prepared to deliver a speech at the 1851 National Woman's Rights Convention in Akron, Ohio, all these thoughts—about the Fugitive Slave Acts, the sidelining of Black women in the abolition and suffrage movements, and her own history—were swirling in her mind. When she arrived, Truth faced a hesitant crowd that was questioning if women's suffrage was worth supporting. Truth's powerful speech, "Ain't I a Woman?," gave them something to think about.

Truth's now legendary lecture showed the unique position that Black women were in as it related to the abolitionist and suffrage movements. She first called out white men and white women who didn't even perceive her as a woman, given their narrow understandings of a female as someone in need of aid:

> That man over there says that women need to be helped into carriages, and lifted over ditches, and to have the best place everywhere. Nobody ever helps me into carriages, or over mud-puddles, or gives me any best place! And ain't I a woman? Look at me! Look at my arm! I have ploughed and planted, and gathered into barns, and no man could head me! And ain't I a woman? I could work as much and eat as much as a man—when I could get it—and bear the lash as well! And ain't I a woman? I have borne thirteen children, and seen most all sold off to slavery, and when I cried out with my mother's grief, none but Jesus heard me! And ain't I a woman?

Truth also spoke about how men discriminated against women simply because they perceived women as inferior, based on their religious beliefs.

> Then that little man in black there, he says women can't have as much rights as men, 'cause Christ wasn't a woman! Where did your Christ come from? Where did your Christ

come from? From God and a woman! Man had nothing to do with Him.

If the first woman God ever made was strong enough to turn the world upside down all alone, these women together ought to be able to turn it back, and get it right side up again! And now they is asking to do it, the men better let them.

It was a fiery speech that resounded through abolition circles, especially among fellow Black women. They were building a baseline for support for abolition and suffrage because they were doubly impacted by lack of freedom. Still, in doing so, in lobbying for their rights, Black abolitionist-suffragists faced a high level of discrimination, right down to questioning their very identity. Despite her speech and her commitment to womanhood, some men wondered if the strong, more than six-foot-tall Sojourner Truth even really *was* a woman. In 1858, during a meeting in Silver Lake, Indiana, someone accused her of being a man: Sojourner Truth opened her blouse and flashed her breasts. Truth's work brought her into the company of white abolitionists, including Mott and Stanton, who considered her an equal and themselves an ally to Truth's cause. That level of solidarity didn't last.

THREE

The Negro Hour Is Upon Us

More than twelve years had passed since the Seneca Falls Convention of 1848, and though there were still activists dedicated to the cause, women's suffrage had begun taking a back seat to an emerging national conflict: the Civil War.

By February 1861, seven states in the South had seceded from the United States and formed the Confederate States of America after Abraham Lincoln, who had a complicated relationship with slavery, was elected president. Though there were a number of reasons why the United States and the Confederate States of America went to war, slavery or a fight over the "proper status of the negro in our form of civilization" was the root cause of the conflict.

The Civil War put woman suffragists in an awkward position: After convening annually for ten years, Elizabeth Cady Stanton and another formidable suffragist, Susan B. Anthony, made the difficult decision to suspend women's rights conventions and put all their efforts and resources toward ending slavery. During the war, Anthony and

Elizabeth Cady Stanton (1815–1902) and Susan B. Anthony (1820–1906) were two of the most famous champions of the American suffrage movement. They met at an anti-slavery meeting in Seneca Falls in 1851 and spent the next five decades working together for women's suffrage and reforms. Together they created the National Woman Suffrage Association, edited the Revolution, and stirred "up the world to recognize the rights of women."

Stanton combined forces to create the Women's Loyal National League (WLNL), an organization that raised money and petitioned state governments to abolish slavery. When Anthony announced the WLNL, she also said, "There is great fear expressed on all sides lest this shall be made a war for the negro. I am willing that it shall be. It is a war which was begun to found an empire upon slavery, and shame on us if we do not make it one to establish the freedom of the negro." Black woman suffragists were more heavily involved in the war effort itself. Sojourner Truth helped the Union Army recruit both enslaved and free Black people to join the effort to defeat the Confederate Army. Harriet Tubman worked as an army nurse, cook, and laundress, and eventually traversed South Carolina as a spy. Mary Elizabeth Bowser, who had been freed from slavery, also worked as a spy. She infiltrated the Confederate White House by passing as a slave working there and gathered information, which she shared with the Union forces.

Four long and bloody years later, the Union won the Civil War in 1865 and effectively ended slavery within the United States. Prominent abolitionists and suffragists like Mott, Stanton, and Anthony convened a few weeks after the Civil War ended to reignite their push for suffrage. Instead, in May 1865, the American Anti-Slavery Society shocked Elizabeth Cady Stanton and Susan B. Anthony when its leaders decided to prioritize citizenship rights and voting rights for formerly enslaved men. Wendell Phillips, the president of the AASS, declared in that first post–Civil War meeting that "we must up take but one question at a time, and this hour belongs exclusively to the negro." Elizabeth Cady Stanton and Susan B. Anthony couldn't believe that women's suffrage was taking a back seat once again. Anthony expressed as much in subsequent letters to Phillips. However, nothing she said could sway him. The AASS would support an amendment which would grant Black men the right to vote; women's suffrage would have to wait.

Harriet Tubman, shown here in the 1870s, was integral to helping the Union Army spy on enemy forces.

In May 1866, the first National Woman's Rights Convention since the Civil War convened in New York City. Both Black and white women attended. Frances Ellen Watkins Harper, who had begun traveling throughout the United States delivering speeches about abolition, was a natural fit to appear at the New York convention. She delivered a jaw-dropping speech about Black women being treated as equals in the suffrage movement:

> I do not believe that giving the woman the ballot is
> immediately going to cure all the ills of life. I do not
> believe that white women are dew-drops just exhaled

from the skies. I think that like men they may be divided into three classes, the good, the bad, and the indifferent. The good would vote according to their convictions and principles; the bad, as dictated by preju[d]ice or malice; and the indifferent will vote on the strongest side of the question, with the winning party.

You white women speak here of rights. I speak of wrongs. I, as a colored woman, have had in this country an education which has made me feel as if I were in the situation of Ishmael, my hand against every man, and every man's hand against me. Let me go tomorrow morning and take my seat in one of your street cars—I do not know that they will do it in New York, but they will in Philadelphia—and the conductor will put up his hand and stop the car rather than let me ride.

The women at the 1866 convention were committed to getting the vote for everyone, so they formed the American Equal Rights Association (AERA) to "secure Equal Rights to all American citizens, especially the right of suffrage, irrespective of race, color, or sex." Sojourner Truth was unwavering in her support of women being allowed to vote. "I feel that I have the right to have just as much as a man. There is a great stir about colored men getting their rights, but not a word about the colored women; and if colored men get their rights, and colored women not theirs, the colored men will be masters over the women, and it will be just as bad as it was before."

In a February 1869 issue of the *Revolution*, a weekly women's rights newspaper, Susan B. Anthony laid out exactly why she disagreed with the Fourteenth Amendment: "The old anti-slavery school say

POSTWAR AMENDMENTS

In the years after the Civil War ended, as part of a larger effort to make life more equitable for Black people who'd been newly freed, there were three pieces of legislation passed, including one that provided Black men with the right to vote. These are known as the Reconstruction Amendments to the US Constitution.

THIRTEENTH AMENDMENT (PASSED AND RATIFIED 1865)
The Thirteenth Amendment officially outlawed slavery in the United States, though it included the caveat that slavery and involuntary servitude could be a punishment for a crime, the amendment ended slavery in its traditional form.

FOURTEENTH AMENDMENT (PASSED 1866, RATIFIED 1868)
The Fourteenth Amendment guaranteed all people born and naturalized in the United States the right to life, liberty, property, and "equal protection of the laws." As a part of this amendment, however, representatives and those who elect them had to be male, at least twenty-one, and US citizens. Adding in the word "male" immediately sparked outrage among woman suffragists who considered that a slight to their cause.

FIFTEENTH AMENDMENT (PASSED 1869, RATIFIED 1870)
The Fifteenth Amendment is the third and final Reconstruction Amendment. It gave voting rights to Black men, noting that the "vote shall not be denied or abridged by the United States or by any State on account of race, color, or previous condition of servitude." This did not include a mention of "gender," which allowed women to continue being discriminated against at the ballot box.

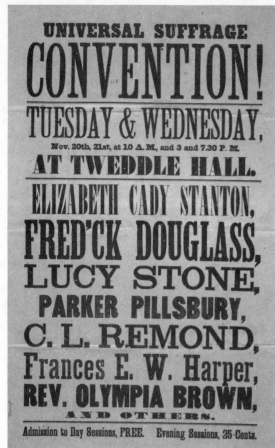

A flyer for the 1866 National Woman's Rights convention.

[sic] women must stand back and wait until the negroes shall be recognized. But we say, if you will not give the whole loaf of suffrage to the entire people give it to the most intelligent first. If intelligence, justice, and morality are to have precedence in the Government, let the question of woman be brought up first and that of the negro last." Anthony's statement was offensive because it declared that African Americans were not as intelligent, just, or moral as women—and Anthony meant white women—so therefore, women should be granted suffrage before Black people. Anthony then famously said, "I will cut off this right arm of mine before I will ever work or demand the ballot for the Negro and not the woman."

One year later, the question of "whose equality, whose suffrage" got even more intense. On February 3, 1870, Congress ratified the Fifteenth Amendment, which stated that "the right of citizens of the United States to vote shall not be denied or abridged by the United States or by any State on account of race, color, or previous condition of servitude." Stanton, Anthony, Mott, and others saw the exclusion of women from this amendment as a form of betrayal, a way of creating inequality between the sexes.

In an effort to encourage white male politicians to reject the Fifteenth Amendment, some white woman suffragists argued that giving Black men access to the ballot box would endanger white politicians' stronghold on politics. Or as Belle Kearney, a suffragist from Mississippi and the daughter of a slaveholder, put it: "The enfranchisement of women would insure immediate and durable white supremacy, honestly attained, for upon unquestioned authority it is stated that in every southern State but one there are more educated women than all the illiterate voters, white and black, native and foreign, combined."

At this same time, many men in the South had begun discussing "the negro problem" or the ongoing voting efforts of Black men, which really had an impact on elections in the South. So Henry Blackwell, one of the founding members of the American Woman Suffrage Association and the Republican Party, made what seemed at the time to be a controversial suggestion: Appeal to the racism of Southerners. In other words, he wanted to convince politicians, especially in Mississippi, that giving "educated women," which was code for white women, the right to vote would dilute the power of the Black vote. Southerners were concerned about how their society was changing as more Black people gained political and social power, and Blackwell's proposal really played on those fears, as he said in a letter addressed to the Southern state legislatures in 1867. "Your 4,000,000 of Southern white women will counterbalance your 4,000,000 of negro men and women, and thus the political supremacy of your white race will remain unchanged. . . . If you are to share the future government of your States with a race you deem naturally and hopelessly inferior, avert the social chaos, which seems to you so imminent, by utilizing the intelligence and patriotism of the wives and daughters of the South."

The question of whether women had to wait for Black men to get the vote first was so divisive that it split the women's suffrage movement into two groups. Despite Harper's rousing speech at the 1866 convention, Stanton and Anthony remained committed to fighting for female suffrage, even if it came at the expense of the Black women in their ranks. They led the National Woman Suffrage Association (NWSA), which opposed the Fifteenth Amendment because it did not give women the vote. The American Woman Suffrage Association (AWSA), led by abolitionist-suffragist Lucy Stone, backed the Fifteenth Amendment. For his part, Frederick Douglass supported the AWSA because he believed that helping Black men secure citizenship should be a top priority as backlash against the Civil War arose. Still, even in his support, Douglass excluded Black women, saying that only when women are "hunted down

The Revolution was the National Woman Suffrage Association's weekly newspaper. The masthead included the motto "Men, their rights and nothing more: Women, their rights and nothing less." NWSA founders and Revolution editors Susan B. Anthony and Elizabeth Cady Stanton accepted funding for their newspaper from George Francis Train, a wealthy, eccentric entrepreneur who opposed suffrage for Black men. During a debate in Ottawa, Kansas, in the 1860s, Train is credited with saying, "Woman first, and negro last, is my program."

through the cities of New York and New Orleans" and "dragged from their houses and hung upon lampposts" could they have an "urgency to obtain the ballot equal to our own." What did this mean, especially since Douglass assumed in his statement that women's right to vote—including Black women's right—wasn't as vital as his own? What about the concerns and needs of Black woman suffragists?

When the Fifteenth Amendment was ratified on February 3, 1870, the racism already bubbling among suffragists reached full boil. Legally, the Fifteenth Amendment extended the right to vote to men, including Black men and men of color, and that infuriated many prominent suffragists. Suffragist leader Anna Howard Shaw argued, "You have put the ballot in the hands of your Black men, thus making them political superiors of white women. Never before in the history of the world have men made former slaves the political masters of their former mistresses!"

Where, though, did this split and turmoil leave Black women who fought for both abolition and suffrage? For Frances Ellen Watkins Harper, the cause of abolition was stronger and more viable than that of suffrage for women. She said that centering white women in the fight for suffrage only led to "airy nothings and selfishness." Black people needed the right to vote—even if Black men were the only ones with access to the ballot box.

Educator, activist, and suffragist Anna Julia Cooper, who later became a prolific writer, was in the middle. Though Cooper wanted Black men to have access to the ballot box, she was most concerned about where the Fifteenth Amendment would leave Black women, who, in her estimate, made all causes "one and universal." She later said, "We take our stand on the solidarity of humanity, the oneness of life, and the unnaturalness and injustice of all special favoritisms, whether of sex, race, country, or condition. If one link of the chain be broken, the chain is broken."

After the Fifteenth Amendment was ratified in 1870, Black men quickly began exercising their right to vote. They voted in waves for Republicans—the party of the late President Abraham Lincoln, who had signed the Emancipation Proclamation. Black men became a

ANNA JULIA COOPER

Anna Julia Cooper (1858–1964), who was born enslaved on a plantation in Raleigh, North Carolina, embraced both the argument that suffrage was important and the idea that Black women should uplift their race. Her father is believed to be George Washington Haywood, a white attorney who owned both Cooper and her mother, Hannah Stanley Haywood. Though Cooper toiled as a domestic servant in her owner/father's home, from a very early age it was clear that she was gifted and would benefit from a formal education.

Cooper was nine years old when the Civil War ended. She received a scholarship to Saint Augustine's Normal School and Collegiate Institute in Raleigh, which was founded to teach skills to formerly enslaved people and their families. While Cooper was grateful to be receiving a formal education, which eluded many other Blacks during her time, she was also dissatisfied with the way that girls were separated from boys at Saint Augustine's.

Cooper was ambitious and bright, and felt stifled at Saint Augustine's. Female students were funneled into the "ladies' course," which prevented women from taking the higher-level classes that prepared male students to either become ministers or attend good four-year colleges. Cooper wanted in on that, so she decided to petition Saint Augustine's to take the classes that her male classmates were taking. She won that fight.

When Cooper arrived at Oberlin College in 1881, she'd already tutored children really influential voting bloc in the South. More than seven hundred thousand African Americans registered to vote between 1870 and 1871. They significantly reshaped state houses, governorships, and the offices of secretary of state, district attorney, sheriff, mayor, and other officials on the local and state level. Fourteen Black men were in the House of Representatives by 1877 and there were two Black male

and become an English and history teacher, but Oberlin still wanted her to take a "ladies' course" instead of a "gentlemen's course." Again, Cooper fought to be included with her male classmates, and again, she won that battle. It wasn't just that Cooper knew she had the intellectual chops to keep up with men; she believed that "intellectual development, with the self-reliance and capacity for earning a livelihood which it gives," would allow more women to become self-sufficient so they wouldn't have to rely on men.

Anna Julia Cooper earned a master's degree in mathematics from Oberlin. She moved to Washington, DC, to teach math and science at the M Street High School, where she was committed to imbuing the Black students with her own high level of confidence. She was also committed to writing about her experiences of being doubted by educators, people in her community, and others who believed that Black people were in any way inferior to white people. She created the Colored Women's League of Washington in 1892, which came under the umbrella of the National Federation of Afro-American Women, and later organized the first Young Women's Christian Association (YWCA) chapter for Black women who weren't being allowed to join other YWCA chapters.

Despite all the good work Cooper was doing, she still faced backlash, particularly from white teachers at the M Street High School. She was fired in 1906, but then decided that further educating herself was as important as educating the next generation of Black leaders and thinkers. As Cooper once said, "I constantly felt (as I suppose many an ambitious girl has felt) a thumping from within unanswered by any beckoning from without." In 1924, at the age of sixty-six, Anna Julia Cooper graduated from the University of Paris with her PhD, making her only the fourth Black woman in the United States to graduate from a doctoral program.

senators from Mississippi who "remov[ed] property requirements for voting," "abolished the medieval system of imprisoning people for debt," and "established statewide free public school systems."

From 1871 to 1877, Black people in the South achieved great things, both inside and outside of politics—until President Rutherford B. Hayes decided to withdraw the remaining federal troops from the South. These US troops had enforced the Fourteenth and Fifteenth Amendments, paving the way for Black men to register to vote without being intimidated or met with violence. Hayes's removal of the troops in March 1877 was political dealmaking that followed the controversial presidential election of 1876. It cleared the path for widespread discrimination. That same year, Georgia passed a poll tax that required Black voters to pay to vote. If they couldn't pay the tax, they were turned away at the polls; voter turnout was reduced to 10,000 voters out of an eligible 369,511 Black voters in Georgia. Other states, such as South Carolina, instituted literacy tests: Voters had to prove they could read in order to vote. Before the end of the Civil War, it had been illegal for enslaved people to learn to read and write. Between 40 and 60 percent of Black voters were illiterate at the time, compared to between 8 and 18 percent of whites. Literacy tests effectively stopped many Black people from voting as well. Southern states, beginning with Mississippi, formalized these barriers in their state constitutions.

In 1887, the US Senate rejected a proposal from the National Woman Suffrage Association for a constitutional amendment that would give women the vote. At that time, it was literally impossible to pass any constitutional amendment in Congress without "yes" votes from Southern senators. When the NWSA proposed their women's suffrage amendment in 1887, thirty-four of the "no" votes came from Southern senators.

Ironically, the Senate's rejection of a suffrage amendment helped bring together the two leading rival women's suffrage organizations, the National Woman Suffrage Association and the American Woman Suffrage Association. The NWSA and the AWSA had taken different sides on

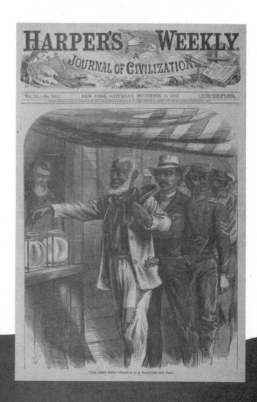

VOTING IN THE SOUTH

After the ratification of the Fifteenth Amendment, Southern states saw an increase in the number of registered voters. When federal troops were withdrawn, however, those numbers dropped dramatically:

- There were 130,344 Black people registered to vote in Louisiana in 1896. By 1900, that number dropped to 5,320, and by 1904, it had declined to 1,718 registered Black voters.

- In 1883, there were 3,742 registered Black voters in Alabama, though there were more than 100,000 people registered to vote in the state.

- In South Carolina, there were 92,081 Black voters registered in 1876. This number dropped to 2,823 by 1898.

- Mississippi had 52,705 registered Black voters in 1876. By 1898, only 3,573 Black people remained on the voter rolls.

the Fifteenth Amendment. They also focused on different strategies to achieve suffrage. The AWSA favored a state-by-state change in laws; the NWSA lobbied for a federal amendment. By 1887, members of both groups felt stalled and frustrated, so Susan B. Anthony and Rachel Foster, a young member of the NWSA, traveled to Boston to meet with Lucy Stone, one of the leaders of the AWSA, and her daughter, Alice Stone Blackwell. They discussed merging their organizations with the sole focus of passing an amendment that would allow women to vote. By January 1889, after a long round of negotiations, Anthony, fellow suffragist Elizabeth Cady Stanton, and other members of these various organizations released an "Open Letter to the Women of America" that announced their decision to work together.

As part of their agreement, the National American Woman Suffrage Association (NAWSA) decided to focus only on suffrage, so there was no commitment to ending discrimination, poverty, lynching, or any of the other urgent issues that mattered to Black women. The NAWSA's single focus allowed them to "ignore the priorities of Black women, an expedient tactic designed to bring in white southern women who did not relish the idea of encouraging Black women to vote." Still, Black women retained their membership in the NAWSA and continued working on suffrage. But they also started forming their own organizations to address their issues.

By the early 1900s, the NAWSA's membership ranks had steadily grown from seven thousand members to two million, which also expanded the organization's political influence. Susan B. Anthony, who led the NAWSA at that time, knew that welcoming more Southern women into their fold would increase the likelihood of Congress passing a suffrage amendment. Although Anthony had friendly relationships with Frederick Douglass, Frances Ellen Watkins Harper, and other Black suffragists, she was also committed to the cause of suffrage at any cost. She relented and reluctantly supported the NAWSA's Southern strategy. Anthony and the NAWSA began actively recruiting women like Kate Gordon, a highly educated and wealthy suffragist from an elite Southern family who believed that the best way to gain suffrage was to play on the South's fear of "negro domination." Anthony also welcomed influential women like Belle Kearney and Laura Clay, who held similar white supremacist views, into the NAWSA.

The NAWSA really leaned into this Southern strategy and shifted their messaging from gaining suffrage for all women to convincing state legislatures to extend voting rights only to educated, taxpaying women. This, as Kate Gordon said, was the "only honorable solution of white supremacy in the South." After Gordon convinced Louisiana's Constitutional Convention to include the clause, "All taxpaying women shall have the right to vote in person or by proxy on all questions of taxation," the NAWSA allowed her to travel through Southern states on their behalf, encouraging other educated white women to join the movement. For Black woman suffragists, education took on an entirely different meaning.

FOUR

The Rise of Black Women's Suffrage Clubs

While so many white suffragists were trying to separate themselves from Black women, journalist, newspaper owner, and activist Ida B. Wells-Barnett knew all too well that it was impossible for Black women to separate suffrage from the other issues they faced in the 1890s. Racial segregation and discrimination had a firm grip on the South; Black people in the South were shut out of economic opportunities, because they were discriminated against by their prospective employers or offered lower wages. And in 1896, the Supreme Court even ruled that "separate but equal" facilities were constitutional. Public bathrooms, schools, restaurants, water fountains, swimming pools, buses, and trains were segregated, meaning that Black people and other people of color had to use different public facilities from white people, and though they were certainly separate, those for people of color were also older, more run-down, and never equal. Daring to use a "whites only" facility was not only illegal, it could also prove to be deadly.

IDA B. WELLS-BARNETT

Ida B. Wells-Barnett (1862–1931) was born to parents who were enslaved in Holly Springs, Mississippi, and from childhood, she understood the odds stacked against her. After the Civil War emancipated her family, both of her parents became involved in local politics, and encouraged their children, including Wells-Barnett, to become formally educated. "Our job was to go to school and learn all we could," she later said. When she enrolled at Rust College, she was expelled for starting a fight with the school's president. After her parents died from yellow fever, Wells-Barnett moved from Mississippi to Memphis, Tennessee.

On a warm September day in 1883, the then twenty-one-year-old Wells-Barnett boarded a train in Memphis, took her seat, and began reading a book. She purposefully sat in the "whites only" section of the train; when the conductor asked her to move to the "colored" car, she refused. The conductor grabbed her and tried to remove her by force—Wells-Barnett bit him on the hand. "I had braced my feet against the seat in front and was holding to the back," she later recalled in her autobiography. "As he had already been badly bitten, he didn't try it again by himself."

The conductor and two other passengers tore Wells-Barnett's dress and almost ripped off one of her sleeves. It took all three men to make her leave her seat. And she still didn't move to the "colored" car. Instead, Wells-Barnett exited the train and, after discussing it with her family and friends, decided to file a lawsuit against Chesapeake, Ohio, and Southwestern Railroad for segregating their train cars. Surprisingly, Wells-Barnett won $500 in the lawsuit, though the verdict was eventually overturned by the Tennessee Supreme Court. It was one of her first acts of defiance; it also ignited her journalism career. R. N. Countee, the owner of the *Living Way*, a weekly religious newspaper in Memphis, asked Wells-Barnett to write a column about her lawsuit against the Southwestern Railroad.

Wells-Barnett's column, which she wrote under the pseudonym "Iola," was wildly popular and picked up by other African American newspapers throughout the United States.

In 1889, a local Memphis newspaper, *Free Speech and Headlight*, invited her to become a columnist. Wells-Barnett had one condition: She had to be made an equal co-owner of the paper. The other two owners agreed. Under her leadership, the *Free Speech and Headlight*, which eventually became known as the *Free Speech*, reached more than three thousand readers each week.

That same year, Thomas Moss, a well-liked and well-respected business owner, opened the People's Grocery in the "Curve," a mixed-race neighborhood in Shelby County, Tennessee, right outside of Memphis. The People's Grocery quickly became a booming success. Wells-Barnett and other Black Memphians took great pride in having their own grocery store. That all changed on March 2, 1892.

William Barrett, a white grocer who served the same community as the People's Grocery, felt threatened by the success of a Black-owned store. He took it personally when a group of Black and white children got into a fight after they'd played a game of marbles near Moss's grocery. Both Moss and Barrett tried to stop the fight; Barrett got clubbed in the head during the melee. He accused Moss and Calvin McDowell and Will Stewart, two other Black men who worked at the People's Grocery, of assaulting him. Barrett brought a police officer to the People's Grocery. The three Black men were arrested for the melee. They never made it to a trial. Moss, McDowell, and Stewart were dragged out of their jail cells by a mob of seventy-five white men, driven to a railroad yard, and shot to death. McDowell was also brutally butchered: His face and neck had holes big enough to fit a man's fist in them.

These men's savage deaths ignited something in Wells-Barnett: She not only wanted to raise awareness about mob violence against Black people in the South, but also to encourage other Black people to move to different cities where they'd receive the support they deserved.

Wells-Barnett encouraged Memphians to leave behind the violence of the South, move west, and start new lives for themselves in places where they would be safe and wanted. "Hundreds left on foot to walk four hundred miles between Memphis and [Oklahoma]," she said during a speech in 1893. "A Baptist minister went to the territory, built a church, and took his entire congregation out in less than a month. Another minister sold his church and took his flock to California, and still another has settled in Kansas. In two months, 6,000 persons had left the city and every branch of business began to feel this silent resentment of the outrage, and failure of the authorities to punish lynchers." While Wells-Barnett was away from Memphis delivering this speech, a mob of white supremacists descended on the *Free Press*. They burned her newspaper office to the ground.

Ida B. Wells-Barnett then moved to Chicago, Illinois, a bustling Midwestern city. She was a part of an early wave of Black people who migrated from the South to Chicago, which welcomed over five hundred thousand Black Southerners between the late 1800s and 1950. Soon after Wells-Barnett arrived in the city, she met Ferdinand L. Barnett, a civil rights activist, attorney, and the founder of Chicago's first Black newspaper, the *Conservator*. He invited Wells-Barnett to write a column for the paper. Their working relationship soon blossomed into a romance, a marriage, and then a partnership that included Wells-Barnett becoming a partial owner of the *Conservator*. In quick succession, Wells-Barnett gave birth to four children, and though she split child-rearing and household duties with Ferdinand, her growing family still had to be more of a priority than traveling the country and delivering speeches about passing an anti-lynching resolution and women's suffrage.

Around this time, Wells-Barnett was also making the difficult decision to focus her activism strictly on Chicago and on raising her children and supporting her husband, Ferdinand. While slowing down wasn't ideal, it did give her time to write more and think more deeply about the connection between suffrage and lynching. In 1910, she wrote "How Enfranchisement Stops Lynching" for *Original Rights Magazine*, and explained that African Americans would always be treated unfairly as long as they were stopped from voting. "The Negro has been given separate and inferior schools because he has no ballot," she wrote. "He therefore cannot protest against such legislation by choosing other law makers, or retiring to private life those who legislate against his interest." In her view, "with no sacredness of the ballot there can be no sacredness of human life itself."

Invoking her power as a journalist and her ability to reach a wide audience, Wells-Barnett drew attention to issues of segregation and to a bigger problem: lynching. The act of violent white mobs murdering Black people, usually by lynching or hanging, was rampant in the South. Black people were lynched for everything from not calling a white man "sir" to dating a person from a different race to being falsely accused of stealing from a store or raping a white woman. In 1892 alone, more than 160 Black people were lynched. (In total, more than 4,000 African Americans were lynched in twelve Southern states between 1877 and 1950.) Wells-Barnett, co-owner and writer for the *Free Speech and Headlight* newspaper in Memphis, Tennessee, began a fierce public crusade.

Wells-Barnett wanted white suffragists to take lynching as seriously as she did, especially after one of her close friends and two members of her Memphis community were murdered by a white mob.

> I have no power to describe the feeling of horror that
> possessed every member of the race in Memphis when
> the truth dawned upon us that the protection of the law
> which we had so long enjoyed was no longer ours; all this
> had been destroyed in a night, and the barriers of the
> law had been down, and the guardians of the public peace
> and confidence scoffed away into the shadows, and all
> authority given into the hands of the mob, and innocent
> men cut down as if they were brutes—the first feeling was
> one of utter dismay, then intense indignation.

These brutal murders galvanized Wells-Barnett. She was shaken, but also energized to raise awareness about how Black families throughout the South were being terrorized by lynching. Wells-Barnett, a five-foot-tall woman with no fear, decided to buy a gun to protect herself, and began traveling the United States to deliver speeches, write newspaper articles, and publish pamphlets about the horrors of lynching.

Wells-Barnett got a lot of pushback, especially from Frances Willard, the president of the Women's Christian Temperance Union. The WCTU was an influential reform organization that wanted to create a "sober and pure world" by banning the legal sale of alcohol, which was seen as the source of many social problems, especially ones that impacted women and children. The WCTU was the most powerful women's organization of the nineteenth century; one of the issues they took up was suffrage.

But as she sought re-form and rights for women, Willard also spoke nega-tively about Black people in America. In an 1890 in-terview with the *New York Voice*, she said that " 'Better whiskey and more of it' is the rallying cry of great, dark-faced mobs," and that "the safety of [white] women, of childhood, of the home, is menaced in a thousand localities." In that same in-terview, Willard also said, "I pity the southerners . . . The

Frances Willard (1839–1898) once said, "An average colored man when sober is loyal to the purity of white women; but when under the influence of intoxicating liquors the tendency in all men is toward a loss of self-control, and the ignorant and vicious, whether white or Black, are most dangerous characters."

problem on their hands is immeasurable. The colored race multiplies like the locusts of Egypt." She also referred to Black Americans as "alien-illiterates" who could "neither read nor write, whose ideas are bounded by the fence of his own field and the price of his own mule."

Willard's comments infuriated Wells-Barnett, who had traveled to Britain to attend a lecture that Willard was giving in London on May 9, 1894. Wells-Barnett interrupted the event, reading from Willard's interview with the *New York Voice* and asking the audience why white women didn't take lynching as seriously. Both women were later interviewed by the *Westminster Gazette*. Willard claimed that Wells-Barnett was hurting her own cause by alienating white suffragists. She claimed that Wells-Barnett had "put an imputation upon half the white race in this country that [was] unjust, and saving the rarest exceptional instances, wholly without foundation."

Wells-Barnett and Willard continued to disagree in newspaper interviews and articles. Willard eventually convinced the WCTU to pass an anti-lynching resolution because, as she said during an 1893 address, "Our duty to the colored people have [*sic*] never impressed me so solemnly as this year when the antagonism between them and the white race have [*sic*] seemed to be more vivid than at any previous time." But despite condemning lynching, her wording also reflected and upheld the idea that whites needed to be protected from Black people. She she still considered herself a "true lover of the Southern People," as she told the *New York Voice*, so she continued being friends with other Southerners who believed in and carried out lynchings.

Ida B. Wells-Barnett had a good friend, Mary Church Terrell, from her days in Memphis. At the time of the Moss, McDowell, and

Stewart murders in 1892, Terrell was living in Washington, DC, and teaching at the M Street High School. The cruel deaths inspired her to begin working with Wells-Barnett and merge their two important crusades: ending lynching and gaining suffrage.

Mary Church Terrell was not relinquishing her membership in the National American Woman Suffrage Association, even when she felt unwelcomed. Like Wells-Barnett, Terrell wanted to help get women the right to vote and get the suffrage group to focus on the issues facing Black people, including lynching. Unfortunately, the NAWSA leadership didn't share Terrell's vision of addressing racial issues, despite Terrell's "delightful, helpful" friendship with Susan B. Anthony, who was still leading the organization. The NAWSA leaders, including Anthony, still wanted to court Southern women and Southern congressmen because they knew that they wouldn't be able to pass an amendment that would grant women the right to vote without Southern support. Unfortunately, the NAWSA's insistence on satisfying Southerners had a rippling impact for the organization's Black woman members. Though Mary Church Terrell and other Black women still belonged to the NAWSA, local chapters of the organization, especially in the South, began turning prospective Black members away.

It was a scary time for Black members of the NAWSA who watched the suffrage organization refuse to address lynching and, meanwhile, build relationships with women who supported the murderous practice. The NAWSA's Southern strategy determined the site of its convention in 1895: Atlanta, Georgia.

This was the first time an annual NAWSA meeting was held outside of Washington, DC. Augusta Howard, organizer of Georgia's first women's suffrage association, convinced the NAWSA's leadership to move the convention to Georgia. She argued that "until you hold a convention in the South," newspapers in the region would continue to insist that "women do not want the ballot." Howard also told Susan B. Anthony and other NAWSA leaders that if they held a convention in Atlanta, many attendees would "go away with NAWSA membership tickets in their pockets." She delivered on those promises: There was not an empty seat in Atlanta's DeGive's Grand Opera House when the NAWSA convention arrived on January 31, 1895. Suffragist and Georgia native Mary Latimer McLendon opened the 1895 convention with a speech that took direct aim at the Fifteenth Amendment and Black male suffrage: "Men alone, white and Black, have the privilege of meeting in legislative session to make laws to govern women."

It didn't matter to McLendon that most Black men in Georgia and throughout the South couldn't register to vote because state

MARY CHURCH TERRELL

Mary Church Terrell (1863–1954) was born in Memphis, Tennessee, on September 23, 1863, to former slaves who instilled in her the value of education and activism. Her father, an avid businessman, became the first Black millionaire in the South. He sent his daughter to Oberlin College, a small private college in Oberlin, Ohio, where Mary earned both a bachelor of arts degree in classical languages and a master's degree in education.

In 1895, the twenty-two-year-old returned from Europe after studying French, German, and Italian for two years. Mary began dating Robert Heberton Terrell, the principal of the M Street High School in Washington, DC, where she'd later teach, and their newfound love fueled her fight for voting rights and racial equality. Mary Church Terrell became an integral part of the Black women's club movement, serving as one of the leaders of the Colored Women's League of Washington and the president of the National Association of Colored Women. In 1940, Terrell wrote *A Colored Woman in a White World*, a memoir about navigating racism in the United States.

governments had begun passing punitive laws that made it more difficult for them to exercise their voting rights. It also didn't matter that Black suffragists who were members of the NAWSA weren't invited to this convention. What mattered to the NAWSA's leadership was that the 1895 convention had one of the largest turnouts ever. Local newspapers, including the *Atlanta Constitution* and the *Atlanta Journal*, published stories about every speech. The convention's success allowed the NAWSA to "make the Solid South a friend to woman suffrage."

Susan B. Anthony was worried that Black Southern attendees would be discriminated against or even face violence if they attended the conference, so she asked Frederick Douglass, who had spoken at nearly every women's suffrage convention since the first one in

1848, not to attend. "I did not want to subject him to humiliation, and I did not want anything to get in the way of bringing the Southern white women into our suffrage association, now that their interest had been awakened," Anthony later told Ida B. Wells-Barnett.

No Black woman attended the 1895 convention in Atlanta, and the NAWSA allowed members to make speeches that promoted the idea that only people with college degrees should be allowed to vote. Abolitionist Henry Blackwell, who'd joined the suffrage cause after the

Civil War, even said at the convention that African Americans and foreign immigrants were "illiterate citizens" who should not be allowed to vote.

It was a slap in the face for Black NAWSA members who'd supported the organization so far, despite all the racist comments made by white suffragists around the passage of the Fifteenth Amendment. Being shut out of the 1895 convention helped Ida B. Wells-Barnett, Mary Church Terrell, and other Black women realize that they couldn't rely on a white-dominated suffrage organization to help them solve the issues facing their community.

After the 1895 convention, the NAWSA deepened its relationship with Southern chapters, which worried both Wells-Barnett and Terrell further. But their approaches to solving the problem of racism within the suffrage movement were very different.

Wells-Barnett continued her campaign to convince mainstream suffrage leaders that lynching was an issue they should also focus on. In 1895, Wells-Barnett published *The Red Record: Tabulated Statistics and Alleged Causes of Lynching in the United States*. This roughly one-hundred-page pamphlet documented lynchings in the South. Wells-Barnett boldly claimed that many Black men were lynched because they'd been falsely accused of raping white women. She found that two-thirds of all lynchings that occurred as punishment for rape were actually about a consensual (mutually agreed upon) sexual encounter between a Black man and a white woman.

Mary Church Terrell, on the other hand, believed in racial uplift or the idea that if African Americans educated themselves, got really prominent jobs, and carried themselves with respect and dignity, they could avoid racism. Racial uplift wasn't an idea that just Terrell bought into: Many African Americans believed that being formally educated could help Black people better navigate the Northern cities they'd migrated to. It was incredibly rare for Black people to have college degrees in the nineteenth century. After all, Black people were forbidden to learn how to read and write when they were enslaved. In 1860, only twenty-eight African Americans had finished college. By the time Terrell attended Oberlin, that number had increased slightly, but she was still a rarity, and faced a lot of racism and discrimination in the classroom. "While we were reciting our history lesson one day, it suddenly occurred to me that I, myself, was descended from the very slaves whom the Emancipation Proclamation set free," she wrote in her autobiography. "I was stunned. I felt humiliated and disgraced." Terrell resolved to "show those white girls and boys whose forefathers had always been free that she was their equal in every respect."

Like Ida B. Wells-Barnett, Terrell had been a friend of Thomas Moss, who was one of the men lynched in Memphis in 1892. Terrell and Frederick Douglass's appeals to President Benjamin Harrison to produce a public condemnation of lynching failed. That same year, Terrell cofounded the Colored Women's League. The club brought together educated Black women to discuss important issues of the day, including lynching and suffrage.

Women's clubs have been a part of Black communities since slavery ended. Black women "organizing themselves for self-help" included raising money for abolitionist newspapers, working with churches to feed poor families, and creating schools that educated Black children. As lynching ramped up, the need for Black women's clubs to organize around social issues became even more urgent. Members of these Black women's clubs were teachers, doctors, beauticians, social workers, and other professionals, and that's one of the reasons so many of these clubs focused on educating Black children.

Josephine St. Pierre Ruffin (1824–1924), the founder of the Woman's Era *periodical, circa 1902.*

The Woman's Era Club—founded in Boston, Massachusetts, between the years 1892 and 1894, by Josephine St. Pierre Ruffin—was another influential Black women's civic organization. Ruffin, a mixed-race, Boston-born woman, was an anti-lynching activist who maintained a tight friendship with Wells-Barnett and Terrell. Josephine and her husband, George L. Ruffin, an African American lawyer who was one of the first Black men to graduate from Harvard Law School, actively participated in Boston's abolitionist movement, which brought them in close proximity to activists who were fighting for both suffrage and the end of lynching. The Woman's Era Club encouraged its members to do charitable works, improve themselves, and invest in philanthropy. Like Terrell, Ruffin was also dedicated to racial uplift, which she covered in the Woman's Era Club's newspaper, the *Woman's Era*—the first national newspaper created by and for Black women.

After the dustup between Frances Willard and Ida B. Wells-Barnett, Ruffin invited Wells-Barnett to speak at the Woman's Era Club; she also published stories about Willard's perspective on lynching. Ruffin wrote that Willard was "obliged to be politic, and for the Welfare of the WCTU not to antagonize any section of this country" because she was the "head of a tremendous organization." Ruffin, like Wells-Barnett, also accused Willard of endorsing lynching because she

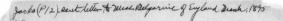

The motto of the Woman's Era was "Help to make the world better." This monthly newspaper for Black women ran from 1894 until 1897. It included interviews with Ida B. Wells-Barnett, Harriet Tubman, and other prominent Black suffragists, as well as news of Black women's clubs.

wanted to protect white women. In an 1895 article titled "Apologists for Lynching," Ruffin challenged Willard, making suffrage impossible to separate from the practice of lynching. "[They are] up to their ears in guilt against Negro women, they offer as their excuse for murdering Negro men, Negro women and Negro children, that white women are not safe from the Negro rapist," she wrote.

Ruffin's and the Woman's Era Club's efforts to raise awareness about lynching and condemn white woman suffragists who supported the practice were models for how other Black women who were creating and joining clubs approached the issues. Suffrage mattered, but not nearly as much as protecting Black communities from violence. In 1895, Willard's presidential address condemned lynching. "It is inconceivable that the WCTU will ever condone lynching, no matter what the provocation, and no matter whether its barbarous spectacle is to be seen in the North or South, in home or foreign countries," she said, which seemingly signaled that she'd gotten the message from Wells-Barnett and Ruffin. Or at least understood that Black women's clubs had a lot of influence, and underestimating their power was a mistake.

In 1895, Josephine St. Pierre Ruffin was contacted by Florence Balgarnie, the secretary of the British Anti-Slavery Society. Balgarnie had received a shocking letter from James W. Jack—a journalist in Missouri and president of the Missouri Press Association—which she shared with Ruffin. In Jack's letter to Balgarnie, he criticized Ida B. Wells-Barnett's approach to anti-lynching. The Missouri journalist claimed that Black women had "no sense of virtue" and were "altogether without character." He also declared that the "Negroes of this country were wholly devoid of morality, the women were prostitutes and were natural thieves and liars." Ruffin was rightfully angry, but she declared Jack's letter too indecent to publish in the *Woman's Era*. Instead, she used it as a rallying call for other Black women who were leading social clubs similar to the Woman's Era Club, such as the Colored Women's League of Washington, the Ida B. Wells-Barnett Club of Chicago, and the Women's Loyal Union of New York. Ruffin circulated copies of the letter to other clubs, and she urged them to join her in convening a national conference in Boston. Fannie Barrier Williams, another influential political activist and educator, believed that Jack's incendiary letter had "stirred the intelligent colored woman of America as nothing else has ever done," and that it was to their advantage to form a united coalition around the issues that mattered most to Black women. This was a departure from the NAWSA, who, in 1899, refused to pass a resolution that would condemn segregated railways.

When the first National Conference of the Colored Women of America convened in Boston on July 29, 1895, more than twenty Black women's clubs from fourteen states were represented. Margaret Murray Washington, the wife of prominent abolitionist and educator Booker T. Washington, encouraged attendees to uplift other Black women who weren't able to improve and develop

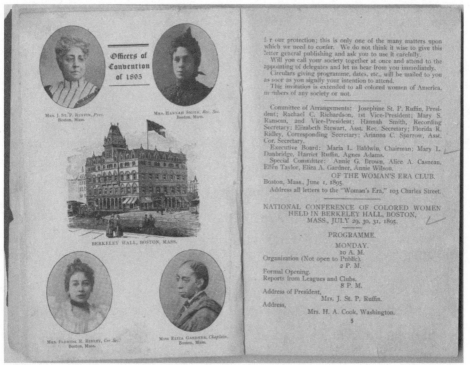

Josephine St. Pierre Ruffin, Hannah Smith, Florida R. Ridley, and Eliza Gardner were the officers of the Colored Women of America convention held in 1895 in Boston, Massachusetts. During the opening remarks, Ruffin said, "We are women, American women, as intensely interested in all that pertains to us as such as all other American women."

their lives because of the lasting stain of slavery. Anna Julia Cooper, the influential educator and scholar and cofounder of the Colored Women's League of Washington, delivered an amazing speech about the importance of Black women organizing around the issues that mattered to them.

Josephine St. Pierre Ruffin, who brought all these groups together in Boston as the Colored Women of America, offered remarks that really gave meaning to why they were all there. "Five years ago we had no colored women's club outside of those formed for the special work; to-day, with little over a month's notice, we are able to call representatives from more than twenty clubs," she said. "It is a good showing, it stands for much, it shows that we are truly American women, with all the adaptability, readiness to seize and possess our opportunities, willingness to do our part for good as other American women."

Ruffin's goal was to help all the women "feel the cheer and inspiration of meeting each other" while also working on "the things that are of special interest to us as colored women, the training of our children, openings for boys and girls, how they can be prepared for occupations and occupations may be found or opened for them, what we especially can do in the moral education of the race with which we are identified, [and] our mental elevation and physical development." Most importantly, they were there as Black women "standing for purity and mental worth," a powerful rebuke to James W. Jack's idea about their immorality.

Josephine St. Pierre Ruffin also had a bigger agenda: She wanted to bring all the Black women's clubs under the same umbrella, so they could share resources and "equip ourselves with knowledge,

THE NACWC'S GOALS

The National Association of Colored Women's Clubs had nine specific objectives at the time:

1. To work for the economic, moral, religious and social welfare of women and children.

2. To protect the rights of women and children.

3. To raise the standard and quality of life in home and family.

4. To secure and use our influence for the enforcement of civil and political rights for all citizens.

5. To promote the education of women and children through the work of effective programs.

6. To obtain for African American families the opportunity of reaching the highest levels of human endeavor.

7. To promote effective interaction with the organization's male auxiliary.

8. To promote interracial understanding so that justice and good will may prevail amongst all people.

9. To hold informative workshops biennially at the organization's National Convention.

The NACWC is still in existence and holds an annual convention in different cities.

sympathy, earnestness for this work." The more than one hundred delegates who attended the first convention agreed. In 1896, Terrell and Ruffin decided to merge their two organizations, the National Federation of Afro-American Women and the National League of Colored Women, into the National Association of Colored Women. In 1904, the organization became known as the National Association of Colored Women's Clubs (NACWC). They created the club's motto, "lifting as we climb," and established the NACWC's goals, including "awaken the women of the race to the great need of systematic effort in home-making." Terrell was elected as the first president of the NACWC.

During her time as president of the NACWC, Terrell also coordinated and edited a monthly newsletter to promote the organization, encouraged members to try to create better kindergartens and nurseries in their communities, and developed places for girls and elderly people to be during the day. What Terrell understood was that voting couldn't be the only issue that Black women focused on. Suffrage was important, but so was the overall uplift of people in the Black community. In 1898, Terrell delivered a blistering speech at the National American Woman Suffrage Association's convention in Washington, DC, that forcefully made this clear. "Not only are colored women with ambition and aspiration handicapped on account of their sex, but they are almost everywhere baffled and mocked because of their race," she said. "Not only because they are women, but because they are colored women, are discouragement and disappointment meeting them at every turn." Terrell also pointed out that Black women were still perceived as "immoral" and "deceptive," even as they fought for suffrage, petitioned state legislatures to grant women the right to vote, and tried to end lynching. "Colored women who are working for the emancipation and elevation of their race know where their duty lies," she declared.

Suffrage was an important goal for Black women's clubs as a tool to help them redress larger issues, such as abuse in the judicial system, being lynched, and not being able to get ahead financially. Getting the right to vote wasn't the end goal; improving the lives of African Americans was.

FIVE

Voting Is Only for Educated Women

By the 1890s, Black women's clubs were booming. More than five thousand Black women joined the seven chapters of the National Association of Colored Women's Clubs, and NACWC President Mary Church Terrell had become the first Black woman to serve on the District of Columbia Board of Education. As the NACWC grew its membership, more and more prominent Black woman suffragists swelled the ranks, which brought a brighter spotlight and increased prestige to local clubs and the larger national organization.

Still, women, especially Black women, were being encouraged by their churches, their husbands, and their families to stay focused and committed to taking care of their homes and their children. Activists like educator Anna Julia Cooper thought they needed to do more.

In 1892, Cooper published her first book, A Voice from the South: By a Black Woman of the South, which is considered one of the earliest books about Black women and feminism. Its overall premise was simple enough: In order to uplift the entire African American community, more African American women had to become formally educated. Education was also going to be a key factor in the suffrage battle.

The NACWC wasn't feminist in terms of how the word is defined today. The organization's primary goal was to help women become better wives and mothers, which members believed in turn would better the entire Black community. As an association, the NACWC excluded women who were considered "lower class" or "unprofessional." The majority of the group's members were professional, middle-class women who considered poor Black people a scourge on the overall image of the Black community. So, in addition to "teaching" poor Blacks how to run their households, create a budget, and raise their children to become better than they were, the NACWC hosted routine "mothers' meetings" in their local chapters to teach women how to prepare different kinds of "healthy" foods, how to take care of their homes, and how to properly care for their children.

In many ways, this approach was demeaning because it assumed that people who weren't middle class and weren't formally educated couldn't properly take care of themselves and their households. And women who couldn't take care of their households surely couldn't or wouldn't be able to make informed choices about electing officials. There was no excuse for this kind of condescension, though Mary Church Terrell and those who followed her as presidents of NACWC—Josephine Silone Yates, Lucy Thurman, and Elizabeth Carter Brooks—didn't see it that way. They genuinely believed that these "mothers' meetings" would help achieve one of the NACWC's goals, which is "to secure harmony of action and cooperation among

JUST LIKE THE MEN!

VOTES FOR WOMEN

VOTES FOR WOMEN

Votes for WHITE women.

A political cartoon, which ran in the New York Tribune *on March 1, 1913, depicts a white suffragist separating herself from a Black suffragist though their goals are similar.*

all women in rising to the highest plane of home, moral, and civil life." In their view, Black communities would remain stagnant and continue being discriminated against as long as poor, working women and their families didn't "better themselves."

At the close of the nineteenth century, Black women were battling on a number of fronts, from the fight to end lynching to finding schools that would admit their children, to facing discrimination in their everyday lives, as on buses where they were forced to sit or stand in the back as they rode to domestic jobs where their employers made them feel invisible. Yet many Black women activists were still fervent suffragists. In their view, getting the right to vote could help them improve the conditions of their communities, bringing in better jobs, ending segregation, and giving their "colored only" schools the resources they needed.

By the time members of the National American Woman Suffrage Association convened in Washington, DC, in February 1898, the organization and the suffrage movement was at a bit of a stalemate. Susan B. Anthony, Elizabeth Cady Stanton, and other NAWSA leaders had organized hundreds of petitions to convince state legislatures to pass suffrage amendments, but they'd had very little success. Of the states the NAWSA had targeted, only four—Wyoming, Colorado, Utah, and Idaho—had adopted measures granting women the right to vote. A number of states, including New York and South Dakota, had failed to pass suffrage resolutions. It was demoralizing that all the suffragists' hard work netted so few results, a reality that was reflected in the somber mood of the conference. There was one attendee, however, who wanted to bring the ongoing tension between the organization's white and Black members to the forefront.

Mary Church Terrell was still one of the NAWSA's most recognizable Black members. She was spending most of her time building up the National Association of Colored Women, which had only been founded two years before (and in 1904 became the NACWC). Terrell

As the National Association of Colored Women's Clubs spread, chapters sprang up all over the country. These women, whose names are unknown, led the Women's League in Newport, Rhode Island, in the early 1900s.

came to the 1898 NAWSA conference to deliver a speech at the behest of Susan B. Anthony, one of her close friends whom she considered to be somewhat of a mentor.

On February 18, 1898, the final day of the conference, Terrell stood behind a podium, turned toward the crowd of primarily white faces, and delivered "The Progress of Colored Women," a blistering speech about the community work that Black woman suffragists were doing without assistance from the NAWSA. The Phyllis Wheatley Club of New Orleans, which was a part of the NACWC, created a training school for Black women nurses since "colored doctors" and nurses were excluded from practicing in most of that city's hospitals. "The daily clinics have been a great blessing to the colored poor,"

NANNIE HELEN BURROUGHS

Nannie Helen Burroughs (1879–1961), an educator, activist, and suffragist, was born to a formerly enslaved couple, John and Jennie Burroughs, in Orange, Virginia. After her father died in or around 1883, Burroughs and her mother relocated from Virginia to Washington, DC, where Nannie was exposed to better educational and social opportunities.

Burroughs excelled in school. When she graduated from the M Street High School, she wanted to pass on the joy she got from learning to poor children who didn't have access to an elite education. She applied for a teaching job in a public school for Black students in Washington, DC, where she'd be able to really have an impact. Though Burroughs was highly qualified, the school preferred light-skinned teachers. She was told she was too dark to teach in DC's public schools, and was turned away.

That traumatic experience completely changed Burroughs's life. Instead of trying to teach at someone else's school, she decided to create her own school for Black girls. In 1908, Burroughs persuaded the National Baptist Convention, an influential organization for Black religious people, to purchase six acres of land for her in northeast Washington, DC. After raising money from a number of wealthy Black donors, Burroughs opened the doors of the National Training

Nannie Helen Burroughs holds the banner (left) in this photo from circa 1905–1915.

School for Women and Girls in 1909. It was one of the first schools solely devoted to educating African American girls and women, and unlike other schools of the time, the National Training School taught girls about more than homemaking. Many Black women of that era didn't have a lot of job opportunities. They were encouraged to take jobs as cooks or maids, but Burroughs wanted them to have access to different kinds of opportunities.

Students at the National Training School were being taught to uplift the Black race by becoming efficient workers and activists. Burroughs led by example on this front. She worked closely with the National Baptist Convention and served as the president of their Women's Convention for more than thirteen years. Thanks to the National Baptist Convention's relationship with the National Association of Colored Women's Clubs, hundreds of Black women joined the National Baptist Women's Convention and participated in their annual meetings. "How the Sisters Are Hindered from Helping," Burroughs's most famous speech, delivered at the 1900 National Baptist Convention, brought her worldwide acclaim and allowed her to travel the United States, speaking about the role of religion in the suffrage movement.

Terrell said, noting that more than two hundred operations had been performed in a sanatorium that the Phyllis Wheatley Club of New Orleans also created, and that they helped the city fight a yellow fever epidemic. Terrell also mentioned the Mt. Meigs Institute, a school created in Mt. Meigs, Alabama, by Cornelia Bowen, a Black woman, to educate many of the more than seven hundred thousand Black people who still lived on plantations in the black belt of Alabama because they couldn't pay to move elsewhere. The Mt. Meigs Institute's students were taught about farming, carpentering, blacksmithing, and other useful trades. Self-reliance, Terrell argued, is what kept the Black communities she served going. "And so, lifting as we climb, onward and upward we go, struggling and striving, and hoping that the buds and blossoms of our desires will burst into glorious fruition ere long," she said at the end of her speech. "Seeking no favors because of our color, nor patronage because of our needs, we knock at the bar of justice, asking an equal chance."

Terrell's speech really resounded among NAWSA members, leading Anthony to invite her to become an ambassador, meaning she'd be an official representative of the organization. While an ambassadorship gave Terrell some power, including being one of the only Black people allowed to attend national meetings, NAWSA leaders still refused to create a subcommittee to focus on the concerns of Black women. So Terrell made the difficult decision over the next few years to turn her attention away from the NAWSA and from fighting explicitly for suffrage to bigger issues facing Black people.

One of the many ways that the NACWC sought to help Black families "better themselves" was to establish kindergartens for poor Black children who might not otherwise have access to a free, public education. In Terrell's view, kindergarten could provide a safe and healthy environment for children and meet the needs of their parents as it related to nutrition, health care, and education. What this meant, overall, was the NACWC wasn't just concerned about getting the right to vote. Though it was important for Black women to gain the vote, if it wasn't coupled with racial uplift, the ending of lynching, or addressing the very real threat of new laws that segregated people based on race, then suffrage wasn't enough.

In 1900, Susan B. Anthony, then eighty years old, retired as the president of the National American Woman Suffrage Association. She'd been the powerhouse behind the organization since its founding in 1890, but she knew it was time for her to pass the baton. Fellow suffragist Carrie Chapman Catt took over as NAWSA president and deepened the organization's commitment to "educated" white women getting the right to vote. Or as Southern suffragist and NAWSA member Kate Gordon boldly stated in a 1901 interview:

> The question of white supremacy is one that will be decided by giving the right of the ballot to the educated, intelligent white women of the South. This is a fact that many of the brightest men in the South are acknowledging today. The white women of the South hold the balance of power. Their vote will eliminate the question of the Negro in politics and it will be a glad free day for the South when the ballot is placed in the hands of its intelligent, cultured, pure, and noble womanhood.

By 1907, Southern suffragists were proposing an amendment to the Mississippi state constitution that would only give white women the right to vote. That seemed to be a step too far for some Northern members of the NAWSA, including Henry Blackwell, who had previously made racist statements about Black suffragists. He told Gordon that this amendment would be a "black eye to the woman suffrage movement all through the North and West" and the NAWSA refused to support the Mississippi amendment.

Even as white suffragists spewed hateful rhetoric in an effort to gain the right to vote, Black suffragists continued slowly, but surely, working on a variety of different issues that impacted their community. While the NAWSA promoted their "educated suffragist" deal that only formally educated women should have access to voting, the National Association of Colored Women's Clubs continued strengthening its motto of "lifting as we climb."

By 1900, other Black woman suffragists, including Terrell's colleague and good friend Anna Julia Cooper, as well as Charlotte Forten Grimké, Ida B. Wells-Barnett, and Mary McLeod Bethune had also turned toward uplifting the race or investing in community programs, like free kindergarten programs, schools, and hospitals, that made life easier for Black people. Terrell turned the National Association of Colored Women Clubs over to educator and journalist Josephine Silone Yates in 1900. Anna Julia Cooper was no longer the principal of the M Street High School, so she traveled to England, France, and other countries in Europe promoting her book, *A Voice from the South: By a Black Woman of the South*, and delivering speeches. Black women's overall disinterest in the NAWSA's approach to suffrage reflected the organization's own stalled plans. Between 1897 and 1909, no state joined the four states that had granted women the right to vote, and Congress wasn't any keener about passing a federal amendment. So Black women, like educator and activist Mary McLeod Bethune, turned their attention back toward their own communities.

Mary McLeod Bethune had a clear vision when she moved with her husband, Albertus Bethune, to Daytona Beach, Florida, in 1904. She wanted to open a school to educate the children of poor Black laborers like her parents and give them the freedom that a formal education had afforded her. In August 1904, she found a rundown building in Daytona Beach, and begged its owner to let her rent it for eleven dollars a month. Bethune put together a hodgepodge of furniture, including crates for chairs and barrels for desks, and supplies that she found in "the city dump and the trash piles behind hotels." Three months later, Bethune opened the doors to the Daytona Educational and Industrial Training School for Negro Girls. Young Black girls paid fifty cents a week to learn everything from science and math to more practical skills, including cooking, sewing, broom-making, and housekeeping. Initially, Bethune had six students, including her son, Albert, who was the only male student, but by the following year, at least thirty girls were enrolled at the school; by 1906, there were more than 250 students. Within a few years, Bethune was able to incorporate higher-level courses, including foreign languages.

While Bethune focused on bettering her Florida community, Ida B. Wells-Barnett and Mary Church Terrell had other plans, including creating a national organization that cared equally about suffrage and ending the inequality that affected so many Black Americans. They would soon get their chance.

On Saturday, July 5, 1908, Clergy "Posey" Ballard, a beloved member of a predominantly white North End neighborhood in Springfield, Illinois, was stabbed to death by an intruder who also attempted to rape his sixteen-year-old daughter. Soon after, another person, Ed Jamison, was stabbed about six blocks away from Ballard's home, though he survived. In the hospital, Jamison described his attacker as a "light-colored negro with a slight mustache." Two local newspapers ran the description, which incited a mob of white men to attack Joe James, a drunken man who was sleeping off a hangover in the same North End neighborhood. The mob dragged James down the street and beat him until the police stepped in, stopped the fight, and arrested James.

Little over a month later, twenty-one-year-old Mabel V. Hallam

MARY MᶜLEOD BETHUNE

Mary McLeod Bethune (1875–1955) was born on July 10, 1875, in a small log cabin in South Carolina to two formerly enslaved people. When her parents were freed after the Civil War, they remained on the plantation and Mary worked along with them. By the time she was nine, she could pick upwards of 250 pounds of cotton every day. She also helped her mother deliver laundry to white families who paid them to clean up after them. Mary was really enthralled by the toys and books she saw in the nurseries of her mother's white employers. One day, one of those employers' children told her that she couldn't read and snatched a book out of her hands. Mary decided to educate herself.

She began walking ten miles every day to attend the Trinity Mission School, a one-room schoolhouse in Mayesville, South Carolina. Since Mary was the only one of her seventeen siblings to attend school, she'd come home and teach her parents, brothers, and sisters what she'd learned. Bethune was smart and invested in her education. She impressed her teacher, Emma Jane Wilson, who helped her secure a scholarship for the Scotia Seminary, a Presbyterian school for Black women in the South and the very first college created for Black women after the Civil War.

Bethune thrived in this environment. She was challenged to evolve her thinking and introduced to different kinds of people and new ideas. The college experience helped her decide what she wanted to do after she graduated in 1893. Inspired by Watson and by the teachers she encountered at Scotia Seminary, Bethune decided to become a teacher as well.

By 1896, she had relocated to Augusta, Georgia, and was teaching at the Haines Normal and Industrial Institute, a Christian school that focused on

preparing girls to take on the world, just as the Trinity Mission School took a special interest in her when she was a child. It was at the Haines Institute that Bethune decided that educating girls and women was one of the best ways to improve conditions for all Black people. "I believe that the greatest hope for the development of my race lies in training our women thoroughly and practically," she wrote to the *New York Times* in 1920. So she started the Daytona Educational and Industrial Training School for Negro Girls.

Her school in Daytona Beach, Florida, expanded so quickly that Bethune had to ride her bike through the muggy streets of Florida, knocking on doors to solicit volunteers and donations, and holding mass bake sales to raise enough money to keep the doors open. Always a champion for education, Bethune eventually met influential political donors who were willing to help her keep the school running. James Gamble, a member of the Procter & Gamble Company, joined Bethune's school board; she traveled to Washington, DC, to secure more funding from wealthy Americans. She befriended future presidents and first ladies, like Franklin D. Roosevelt and his wife, Eleanor Roosevelt, and even secured a $62,000 donation from John D. Rockefeller, one of the most famous and wealthy Americans at that time. Bethune spent the remainder of her life educating Black children. She cofounded the United Negro College Fund in 1944, an organization that gives scholarships and job opportunities to Black students who attend historically Black colleges and universities, and dedicated herself to racial uplift.

was raped and violently assaulted in the North End on August 14. She also accused a Black man, George Richardson, of committing the crime. When Richardson was arrested and thrown in the same jail as James, white mobs descended and attempted to pry the doors open so they could lynch both Black men. Police officers arranged for restaurant owner Harry T. Loper to sneak Richardson and James out of the jail and transport them to another facility about sixty-five miles away to protect them. Though Loper was successful in getting Richardson and James to safety, these same white mobs rioted, burned down Loper's restaurant and other Black-owned businesses, and inflicted violence on Black people in Springfield. Within a week, sixteen people were dead, including nine Black residents. More than one hundred Springfield residents were charged with inciting a riot and murder; the melee shocked the nation. It was a level of violence that many Americans had never seen before, prompting both white and Black people to begin thinking about a civil rights organization that would fight to end lynching and other racial violence.

Ida B. Wells-Barnett, ever the vocal activist, used the 1908 Springfield riot to declare lynching "our national crime" at the National Negro Committee Conference, which was formed explicitly after the riot to bring America's greatest leaders together to discuss the number of social issues plaguing African Americans. "The only certain remedy [to lynching] is an appeal to law," Wells-Barnett declared. "Lawbreakers must be made to know that human life is sacred and that every citizen of this country is first a citizen of the United States and secondly a citizen of the state in which he belongs." Wells-Barnett called for states to prosecute people who participated in lynching. It was a controversial idea that didn't gain traction because many of the people harming others were police officers, judges, legislators, and everything in between, so it was a nonstarter to ask them to arrest and prosecute themselves.

Treating lynching as a crime, however, was a mission that suffragist and journalist Mary White Ovington, labor reformer William English Walling, and activist Henry Moskowitz wanted to get behind. So they traveled to New York City in January 1909 to start creating the National Association for the Advancement of Colored People (NAACP). They invited more than sixty other prominent Americans, including Wells-Barnett, Terrell, and W. E. B. Du Bois—the first African American to earn a PhD from Harvard University—to come together and officially form the organization. It took two years and many compromises, but the NAACP officially became an organization in 1911. Its mission was to "promote equality of rights and to eradicate caste or race prejudice among the citizens of the United States; to advance the interest of colored citizens; to secure for them impartial suffrage; and to increase their opportunities for securing

The NAACP regularly flew a flag at their headquarters in New York City whenever a Black person was lynched in the South.

justice in the courts, education for the children, employment according to their ability and complete equality before law."

While the NAACP was committed to convincing the federal government to pass an anti-lynching law and traveling to the South to both document and try to end racial segregation, there was also a continued focus on suffrage within the organization. In Du Bois's estimation, "votes for women means votes for Black women" because having access to the ballot box would give Black women more control over "the conduct of educational systems, charitable and correctional institutions, public sanitation and municipal ordinances." In Du Bois's view, as well as that of the NAACP, voting was a crucial component of uplifting the Black race.

By the time the NAACP formed, Anna Howard Shaw, a protégé of Susan B. Anthony, had taken over the NAWSA. She attempted to reform the organization's image after racist rhetoric and proposals from Southern members, including her own statements, had soured its reputation, especially among Black members. Shaw was comfortable shutting down the Southern Woman Suffrage Conference's plan to host a segregated conference, and was equally comfortable asking members of the NAWSA to turn over their wedding rings to the organization so they could fund an effort to convince eastern states to consider a suffrage amendment. Her fearlessness seemingly rubbed off on other members of the NAWSA, who not only donated their rings, but also contributed gold nuggets, other pieces of jewelry, and anything of value that could be used. That effort raised thousands of dollars. It also brought more women into the fold of the NAWSA; by 1910, the NAWSA had added more than 117,000 new members.

However, women's suffrage was still a campaign, not yet a reality.

The NAWSA continued calling for a federal amendment, but prioritized persuading individual states to pass suffrage laws. By the time the NAWSA hosted its annual convention in Louisville, Kentucky, on October 19, 1911, only one new state—Washington—had agreed to pass a law that gave women the right to vote. Shaw's goal was to get so many states to pass suffrage laws that the federal government would have no choice but to pass a federal amendment. Shaw had inherited the highly charged question of whether having Black members and delegates could jeopardize that possibility. The NAWSA still believed it needed the support of Southern states to pass a national suffrage amendment.

There was a lot of tension between the NAACP and the NAWSA as the NAWSA approached its 1911 convention. In August, about two months before the convention took place, writer, journalist, and suffragist Martha Gruening requested the NAWSA consider a resolution that would denounce white supremacy and asked for a "colored delegate" to bring the resolution to a vote. Shaw refused both requests, and the resolution was never voted on. "I do not feel that we should go into a Southern State to hold our national convention and then introduce any subject which we know beforehand will do nothing but create discord and inharmony in the convention," Shaw responded to Gruening's request. "I am in favor of colored people voting, but white women have no enemy in the world who does more to defeat our amendments, when submitted, than colored men, and until women are recognized and permitted to vote, I am opposed to introducing into our women suffrage convention a resolution in behalf of men who, if our resolution were carried, would go straight to the polls and defeat us every time."

Apparently, as much as things changed at the NAWSA with Shaw's appointment, they still remained the same. The NAWSA was committed to passing a federal amendment at any cost, including alienating Black members of the NAWSA. Notably, no prominent Black woman suffragist—including Mary Church Terrell, who'd spoken at multiple conventions—attended the 1911 conference. Their attention was still on racial uplift, so W. E. B. Du Bois, who'd begun running the NAACP's newspaper, the *Crisis*, stepped in. In a 1911 editorial for the *Crisis*, Du Bois wrote, "The nemesis of every forward movement in the United States is the Negro question. Witness Woman Suffrage." He then accused Shaw of spreading the "barefaced falsehood" that "all Negroes were opposed to woman suffrage," before concluding that the suffrage movement must begin considering Black women "according to their character and not according to their color." It was a rebuke of the decades the suffrage movement had spent excluding Black women instead of including them and listening to their important concerns.

When word of Du Bois's letter reached Shaw, she responded in a letter that was published in the *Crisis* in 1912. "There is not in the National Association any discrimination against colored people," Shaw wrote. "If they do not belong to us it is merely because they have not organized and have not made application for membership. Many times we have had colored women on our program and as delegates, and, I, personally, would be only too glad to welcome them as long as I am president of the National Association."

Clearly that was not the case, and Du Bois considered Shaw's response "wholly inadequate." The NAACP was also dissatisfied with Shaw's response, and decided that the best way to move forward would be to push the NAWSA to associate the "Black cause with the woman suffrage cause" by submitting a resolution that emphasized that both women and Blacks were "trying to lift themselves out of the class of the disenfranchised." Du Bois and the NAACP believed that the only way to have a real democratic government—where every vote is counted and every person gets a vote—was to guarantee that both Blacks and women were freely able to vote. Du Bois got at the heart of this in a May 1913 editorial titled "Woman's Suffrage," where he wrote, "Let every Black man and woman fight for a new democracy which knows no race or sex."

Shaw listened, to a degree, and invited Du Bois to deliver the keynote speech at the NAWSA's convention in 1912. Still, as Du Bois talked over them and Shaw ignored them, Black women remained on the sidelines of the mainstream suffrage movement—so they created their own organizations.

SIX

Taking It to the Streets

Wells-Barnett agreed with the NAWSA's view that persuading states to pass suffrage amendments would usher in a federal amendment, so she decided to test out this theory in Illinois. As she traversed Chicago's sprawling neighborhoods to speak with ordinary African Americans about suffrage, she found that many of the people she came across didn't know much about the ongoing fight to get women the right to vote.

This fact discouraged Wells-Barnett because the Illinois state legislature had passed a partial suffrage bill in 1891 that gave women over the age of twenty-one the right to vote for school officials. It wasn't full suffrage: Women in Illinois couldn't vote in presidential elections, for example, but they *could* change who represented them locally. They were now able to vote for African American and woman candidates.

Wells-Barnett believed that "we [women] could use our vote

for the advantage of ourselves and our race," but it would be difficult for African American women in Chicago to advocate for politicians who cared about their issues if the women themselves didn't even know what was going on. Wells-Barnett began talking with one of her close friends, Belle Squire, an active member of the suffrage movement, about how they could educate Black women about the important changes that would soon be happening in the state. In January 1913,

In the early 1900s, Ida B. Wells-Barnett slowed her national activism to more closely focus on her family. She and her four children, Herman Kohlsaat Barnett, Alfreda Barnett, Charles Barnett, Ida B. Barnett, are pictured here in 1909.

Wells-Barnett and Squire created the Alpha Suffrage Club. The mandate of the club was to teach more African American women how to use their voice "for the advantage of ourselves and our race" and to provide information about the importance of voting. Wells-Barnett and Squire didn't have many resources, but they were able to organize meetings; within months, the Alpha Suffrage Club had more than two hundred members.

Wells-Barnett created a system where Alpha Suffrage Club members would walk through neighborhoods that were predominantly Black and register voters with the aim of helping elect Chicago's first African American alderman or councilman. She put her plan in motion in 1914, when Hugh Norris, incumbent councilman for the

FANNIE BARRIER WILLIAMS

Fannie Barrier Williams (1855–1944) was born to Anthony and Harriet Barrier—two free African Americans—in Brockport, New York, on February 12, 1855. The Barriers were one of the only Black families in their upstate community, and Fannie became the first African American to earn a degree from the Brockport Normal School (a college) when she graduated in 1870. Williams described her childhood as "sweet and delightful" in an article about her life published in 1904, and said that "there could not have been a relationship more cordial, respectful and intimate that that of our family and the white people of this community."

In many ways, Williams was sheltered, and didn't understand how much discrimination other African Americans faced. She found out when she moved to Hannibal, Missouri, to teach at a school for newly freed African Americans. She was further disturbed when she moved to Washington, DC, at the end of the 1870s to continue teaching African Americans who had moved from the South after the Civil War ended. Though Williams met her husband, S. Laing Williams, in DC, she still felt out of place in a city where African Americans were routinely discriminated against. Fannie faced racism firsthand when she tried to enroll at the School of Fine Arts to study painting and was turned away.

In the early 1880s, Williams and her husband moved to Boston, Massachusetts, so she could study music at the New England Conservatory of Music. Though she was accepted into the Conservatory, she was asked to withdraw when her white classmates threatened to leave if she was allowed to continue studying there. Williams was devastated—and inspired to become an activist.

The Williamses moved to Chicago, and Fannie became really active in organizations like the Hyde Park Colored Voters Republican Club and the Taft Colored League, which were fighting to give women the right to vote, end lynching, and improve life for the city's African American community. Eventually, Williams became the first woman to serve on the Chicago Public Library's board of directors.

Williams was a passionate suffragist. She joined the Illinois Women's Alliance and began traveling throughout the United States making the case for women, especially Black women, to gain the right to vote. Williams, alongside Mary Church Terrell and Ida B. Wells-Barnett, also cofounded the National League of Colored Women in 1893; when the organization merged with another organization to become the National Association of Colored Women in 1896, she remained active and helped run "mothers' meetings" when they began in the early 1900s.

Williams delivered her most famous speech, "The Intellectual Progress of the Colored Women of the United States Since the Emancipation Proclamation," during the Chicago World's Fair in 1893. She made the compelling argument that African American women weren't inferior to other women in any way, and that all women should come together to fight for suffrage. "The hearts of Afro-American women are too warm and too large for race hatred," she said. "Long suffering has so chastened them that they are developing a special sense of sympathy for all who suffer and fail of justice. All the associated interests of church, temperance, and social reform in which American women are winning distinction can be wonderfully advanced when our women shall be welcomed as co-workers, and estimated solely by what they are worth to the moral elevation of all the people."

Fannie Barrier Williams so greatly contributed to the suffrage movement that she was the only African American chosen to eulogize Susan B. Anthony at her funeral in 1906.

Would **YOU** rather have a VOTE than a HUSBAND?

YES says Mrs Belle Squire

NO says Miss Helena Bingham

Suffragist Belle Squire (1870–1939), was born and raised in Illinois and she became a noted activist in the early 1900s. Squire adopted the idea that women being taxed while not being represented in government or able to vote for their representatives violated the Constitution, so she refused to pay taxes on her property in 1910 and encouraged approximately 5,000 women in Cook County, a community in Chicago, to follow suit. In 1911, she published The Woman Movement in America: A Short Account of the Struggle for Equal Rights, *which furthered her "taxation without representation" philosophy, and in 1913, she cofounded the Alpha Suffrage Club with Ida B. Wells-Barnett.*

Second Ward, came up for re-election. During the primary, when voters choose the candidate who lands on the election ballot, Wells-Barnett and the Alpha Suffrage Club threw their support behind local businessman William Randolph Cowan, who was challenging Norris for his seat.

As Wells-Barnett and other members of the Alpha Suffrage Club traveled through Chicago neighborhoods registering voters, they often heard negative comments from men who were opposed to women voting. Some men told the Alpha women that they "ought to be at home taking care of the babies," while others said they were "trying to take the place of men and 'wear their trousers.'" This discouraged many of the Alpha Suffrage Club's canvassers, but Wells-Barnett wasn't deterred. She encouraged those women to return to those same neighborhoods and register more voters. Their persistence paid off: Alpha Suffrage Club members registered 7,290 female and 16,327 male voters by the time the primary happened in February. Unfortunately, their efforts were unsuccessful; though more than three thousand women voted in the Second Ward during the primary, it wasn't enough for Cowan to defeat Norris. However, there was also a silver lining: Cowan had won 45 percent of the vote; he'd only lost by three hundred votes. The newly registered women voters were responsible for that close loss. Most importantly, the Alpha Suffrage Club knew they could register another three hundred voters before the next election.

The Alpha Suffrage Club's successful strategy and voter registration drive grabbed the attention of local newspapers, such as the *Chicago Defender*, which ran a story that said, "The women's vote was a revelation to everyone, and after analysis shows them still actuated by the sense of duty to do more." It also gave Wells-Barnett a new goal to strive for: electing Chicago's first Black alderman. The Republican Party also thought the Alpha Suffrage Club had the ability to achieve this goal. After Cowan's loss, the Republican Party asked local politician Oscar DePriest and Samuel Ettelson, the president of an organization in the Second Ward, to attend an Alpha Suffrage Club meeting and encourage its members to endorse and campaign for their future candidates. Wells-Barnett agreed, but offered one condition: The Republican Party had to nominate an African American candidate for councilman. It was a deal, but now Wells-Barnett had to deal with the NAWSA, and this time, she wouldn't be deterred by the organization's racism.

SEVEN

The Back of the Movement: The Women's Suffrage March

Alice Paul, a twenty-eight-year-old radical and revolutionary suffragist, thought the National American Woman Suffrage Association wasn't doing enough to get the federal government to recognize its proposed suffrage amendment. By 1911, several states, including Colorado, Utah, Idaho, and Washington, had passed laws granting women the right to vote, but the NAWSA was no closer to getting incoming president Woodrow Wilson or Congress to recognize the need for and to do something about a federal women's suffrage amendment. Paul was tired of waiting, and she wasn't interested in traveling around the country trying to convince lawmakers to pass individual state suffrage amendments, while the president and the lawmakers in the capital pretended suffragists were just annoying, buzzing flies who would eventually go away. Direct action—bringing attention to the issues through confrontational and sometimes dangerous activism— was more appealing to Paul.

ALICE PAUL

When Alice Paul (1885–1977) joined the NAWSA in 1910, she'd just returned to the United States after living in London for two years. There she had worked with the Women's Social and Political Union, an organization that was fighting for British women's suffrage. British suffragists, such as Christabel Pankhurst, took a much more radical approach to getting women the vote. These suffragists directly confronted politicians and protested their speeches; they camped out in government buildings as a form of protest; and sometimes turned to more violent protest, such as smashing windows and arson.

Civil disobedience—purposely breaking laws to reveal the unfairness of them—became Paul's preferred method of protesting. Though it led her to being arrested and released seven times and held in jail three times, it also put her in close proximity with other suffragists, like Emmeline Pankhurst—Christabel Pankhurst's mother—and Lucy Burns, who taught Paul how to be an effective activist. Paul and her contemporaries staged hunger strikes when they were incarcerated, which brought more attention to the suffrage cause, but also meant they were subjected to painful forced feedings in prison.

After participating in such intense and extreme activism, Paul thought the NAWSA's passive approach was inadequate and ineffective, and had to be changed. When Paul and Burns returned from London to the United States in January 1910, they wanted to shake the NAWSA out of complacency and make a push for a federal suffrage amendment.

Both women made that suggestion at the NAWSA's annual convention. NAWSA President Anna Howard Shaw and other leaders laughed at them; though their plan was slow, it was steady, and they didn't want to abandon the state-by-state strategy or engage in civil disobedience. In fact, Shaw said that she was "unalterably opposed to militancy, believing nothing of permanent value has ever been secured by it that could not have been more easily obtained by peaceful methods." But Paul and Burns didn't give up, and by 1912, they'd officially joined the NAWSA and were working on a strategy to secure a federal suffrage amendment.

By December 1912, Alice Paul and fellow suffragist Lucy Burns had decided that their first direct action would be a parade down Pennsylvania Avenue in Washington, DC. It would take place on March 3, 1913, the day before Woodrow Wilson's presidential inauguration.

At first, the NAWSA was resistant to their plan. During the NAWSA's annual convention, Paul was told she'd have to raise the money for the parade without any assistance from the organization. This was a big challenge because Paul and Burns and their followers were looking to get women from all over the country to participate. Paul wanted to model her parade after similar suffrage marches that were held in Britain while she was living there, so she knew that getting newspapers to include leaflets about the parade was the best way

The official cover of the program for the 1913 National American Woman's Suffrage Association march.

to advertise it. She created a press office that was responsible for contacting writers and editors at newspapers around the country and convincing them to run positive stories about Paul and the suffrage parade.

Paul also recruited volunteers to contact various suffrage chapters around the country to both donate to the parade and commit to attending. Within two months, Paul had raised $15,000, which would translate to about $360,000 in today's money, and gotten eight thousand women to agree to travel to Washington, DC, to participate in the parade "of fine dignity, picturesque beauty, and serious purpose." She'd also gotten volunteers to create twenty-four floats, recruited nine bands to play during the march, and secured the permits required to shut down Pennsylvania Avenue, which was and still is one of the busiest streets in Washington, DC.

In every way, it seemed that Paul was set to pull off the biggest suffrage march that the United States had ever seen. There was just one thing she'd failed to account for: the role of African American suffragists in the march. In the months leading up to the march, *Women's Journal*, a weekly Boston newspaper founded by Lucy Stone and Henry Blackwell, ran a letter from a reader asking if African Americans would be allowed to participate in the parade. This letter caused a mild panic for Paul, who hadn't considered if Black suffragists would walk in the parade, and what impact, if any, that would have on her goal to convince Woodrow Wilson to back a federal suffrage amendment. She asked fellow parade organizer Helen Gardner to contact the *Women's Journal* and ask its editors to "refrain from publishing anything which can possibly start that [negro] topic at this time" because "the participation of negros would have a most disastrous effect" on the suffragists from the South who'd already agreed to attend the parade. Paul encouraged the parade's organizers to "say nothing whatever about the [negro] question, to keep it out of the papers, [and] to try to make this a purely Suffrage demonstration entirely uncomplicated by any other problems."

When the parade organizers' requests reached Mary Church Terrell, activist Adella Hunt Logan, and Ida B. Wells-Barnett, their response was swift and firm: They were going to participate in the parade. They and other Black women were as invested in suffrage as Paul and other members of the NAWSA. Terrell sent telegrams to Black women's clubs encouraging members to travel to Washington, DC, and march in the parade. Nellie Quander, the president of Alpha

ALPHA KAPPA ALPHA SORORITY

Alpha Kappa Alpha Sorority, Inc., was the first Greek-letter organization created for African American college women. It was started in 1908 on the campus of Howard University, a college that educates Black Americans, by Ethel Hedgeman Lyle. Ethel wanted to create some form of sisterhood at Howard, which was already teeming with fraternities, or organizations that accept male college students, so she enlisted the assistance of one of her teachers, Ethel Robinson. Robinson encouraged Hedgeman to start her own sorority with the purpose of uplifting women on their campus and helping them become more involved in social activism. Hedgeman loved the idea, so she recruited eight other classmates, named the organization Alpha Kappa Alpha, and began the long process of establishing a new sorority on a college campus. By 1911, there were twenty members and the sorority was steadily growing to include more students and refine its mission of doing "service for all mankind." Other chapters soon opened, like the one shown here on the campus of Wilberforce University in Wilberforce, Ohio. Now, more than 120 years after Alpha Kappa Alpha was founded, there are over 200,000 members spread across 992 chapters in the United States, the Caribbean, Canada, and South Africa.

Kappa Alpha, the first sorority for African American women, wrote a letter to Paul because she and her organization wanted to participate, but they wouldn't join in if they were separated from white suffragists in any way.

The Illinois Equal Suffrage Association, which counted Wells-Barnett as one of its members, reached out to Paul to ask if African American marchers would be allowed: They never received an answer. Paul was unsure how to respond. If she allowed Black women to participate in the parade, it could alienate some white women. If she didn't allow Black women to participate in the parade, it could cut Paul off from suffragists who could use their resources to help her and the NAWSA lobby for a federal suffrage amendment. So Alice Paul chose to ignore the conundrum altogether, until seventy-two hours before the 1913 March on Washington was scheduled to begin. That's when the NAWSA intervened, sending a telegram to Paul telling her that "so strongly [urging] Colored women not to march . . .

amounts to official discrimination which is distinctly contrary to instruction from National Headquarters." Paul was also sternly instructed to include Black women in the parade or risk having it called off altogether. It was a complete departure from the NAWSA's typical approach to racial tension, which can be reasoned to mean that explicitly excluding or "officially discriminating against" Black women could have drawn negative attention or led to legal action that the NAWSA didn't want to face.

Despite warnings from the NAWSA and general discontent from other parade organizers, Paul still didn't know how she'd address the inclusion of Black women in the March on Washington. As Paul weighed these options, women across the country packed their suitcases, boarded trains, and started the long trek to Washington, DC. Some suffragists, like the sixteen women dubbed the "suffrage pilgrims," decided to walk from New York to Washington—a journey that took more than twenty-four hours. Eventually, one of the men leading the Quaker section of the march approached Paul and told her that their delegation could divide Black suffragists from Southern suffragists by marching between them, but this would still require separating Black suffragists into their own segregated group.

Wells-Barnett was also packing and preparing to travel to DC. She planned to walk in the parade with the Illinois delegation; but just as the group was about to leave, Grace Wilbur Trout, president of the Illinois Equal Suffrage Association, informed Wells-Barnett that the NAWSA was going to segregate the event. Black suffragists would have to march together at the back of the parade instead of walking with their home state delegation. This news devastated

Wells-Barnett and caused many of the other Illinois delegates to begin debating whether they wanted to attend at all. "If the Illinois women do not take a stand now in this great democratic parade then the colored women are lost," Wells-Barnett said emotionally. Though Trout tried to get the NAWSA to reconsider, they again told the Illinois delegates that they would have to segregate. Wells-Barnett decided to travel to Washington, DC, with the Illinois delegates, but said that she would not take part "unless I can march under the Illinois banner."

At 9:00 a.m. on March 3, 1913, people began arriving on Pennsylvania Avenue, more than six hours before the parade was scheduled to begin. By 3:00 p.m., more than five thousand women had shown up, but they were immediately met with protesters. "Men, many of them drunk, spit at the marchers and grabbed their clothing, hurled insults and lighted cigarettes, snatched banners and tried to climb floats. Police did little to keep order. Observed one of Paul's supporters, 'I did not know men could be such fiends.'" More than one hundred marchers had to be taken to the hospital, and it would take more than an hour for the actual parade to begin.

But finally the parade started, led off by activist lawyer Inez Milholland boldly astride a white horse. The lead banner read: "We Demand an Amendment to the United States Constitution Enfranchising the Women of the Country." Somewhere between five thousand and eight thousand women, wearing white as a symbol of suffrage, or dressed in an array of uniforms that represented the different jobs they held, walked down Pennsylvania Avenue.

When the parade officially got underway, Wells-Barnett was nowhere to be found. Illinois delegates assumed that she'd left because

Ida B. Wells-Barnett was initially segregated from the Illinois delegation at the 1913 March on Washington, but she would not be denied. A photographer at the Chicago Daily Tribune *captured a photo of Wells-Barnett joining her delegation, which ran in the March 5, 1913, edition of the newspaper.*

she didn't want to walk in a segregated delegation, but in actuality, she'd only slipped out of the parade line. She waited patiently and quietly, hiding among the 250,000 spectators watching the parade. When the Illinois delegation got close enough, she jumped back into the procession and marched between two white women who were carrying the Illinois delegation's signage. A photo of Wells-Barnett flanked by two white suffragists appeared in the *Chicago Daily Tribune*, capturing the moment that she defied orders and took her rightful place in history.

Wells-Barnett wasn't the only Black suffragist to ignore orders during the parade. Mary Church Terrell was also at the march. She joined a delegation from Delta Sigma Theta, a newly formed sorority for African American college women, which included its twenty-two founding members. The parade was their first public event, and they took full advantage of the moment.

Despite the violence and the chaos, the suffrage march achieved exactly what Alice Paul aimed for it to: It was on the front page of nearly every newspaper in the United States and had generated enough momentum to get the attention of President Wilson and Congress. The parade marked a significant turning point in the fight for women's suffrage. Within two weeks, Wilson had invited Paul and other suffragists to the White House. Though Paul pushed him during that meeting, he said that it wasn't the right time for a federal suffrage amendment and encouraged her to continue the fight. That's exactly what Paul did.

When Wells-Barnett traveled home from Washington, DC, to Chicago, she was reinvigorated and ready to continue reshaping Chicago's politics so the city's African American communities were better represented. She and the Alpha Suffrage Club picked up where they'd left off, canvassing communities, registering voters, and educating the Second Ward and other predominantly Black communities about the voting process. By 1914, when the councilman position opened again, the Alpha Suffrage Club was ready! They planned to use their political power to turn out the vote and elect the city's first Black elected official.

The Republican Party decided to nominate businessman Oscar DePriest to run as councilman for the Second Ward. Priest was the son of formerly enslaved people from Florence, Alabama. His candidacy also encouraged other African American candidates to run, making it the first time that more than one Black person was running for office in Chicago. As Wells-Barnett had promised, the Alpha Suffrage Club threw its support behind "our young giant Oscar DePriest" and pledged "to leave no stone unturned" as they worked to get him elected. All the club's hard work paid off on February 27, 1914, when DePriest won the primary with 3,194 votes. Black woman voters accounted for one-third of those votes then and again during the general election, when DePriest won with 10,599 votes. It was one of Wells-Barnett's biggest political victories, and set the stage for other cities across the country to make the case that giving women access to the ballot could turn the tide of an election.

For Alice Paul, the end of the parade was just the beginning of her activism to gain women the right to vote throughout the entire country. She left the NAWSA in 1916 because some of the organization's members believed her tactics were too radical, militant, and "unladylike." Paul formed the National Woman's Party and began employing the tactics she'd learned in London. She began directly attacking President Wilson because she thought it was the best way to draw his attention to her cause.

Paul organized the "Silent Sentinels," a group of women, dressed in purple and wearing gold and white sashes, who stood outside of the White House six days a week from January 1917 to June 1919 with protest signs that read "Mr. President—What Will You Do for Woman Suffrage?" and asked how long they'd have to wait before they'd get the right to vote. Day in and day out, no matter if it was sunny, raining, or snowing, women picketed in front of the White House. Mary Church Terrell often joined them, noting that as a Black

The first picket line

below   College Day in the picket line - Feb. 1917

"Silent Sentinels" picket the White House, February 1917.

woman, she was a part of the "only group in this country that has two such huge obstacles to surmount—sex and race."

While Paul and others picketed outside the White House, Black women continued to fight racism inside the suffrage movement itself. In 1915, the *Crisis* published a special issue about suffrage; it included essays from educator Nannie Helen Burroughs, NAACP vice president Mary B. Talbert, and lifelong National American Woman Suffrage Association member Adella Hunt Logan. All of their essays focused on the discrimination they faced as Black suffragists. Talbert wrote that the struggle was twofold, "first, because we are women and second because we are colored women."

The NAWSA's racism toward Black woman suffragists

continued throughout the 1900s, culminating with new president Carrie Chapman Catt refusing to allow the Northeastern Federation of Women's Clubs, an organization for and about Black women, to become a part of the NAWSA in 1919. Catt had long believed that white supremacy would be "strengthened, not weakened, by women's suffrage," so permitting this organization could alienate the white Southern voters they needed to persuade Woodrow Wilson to endorse and propose an amendment. It was the same old story, just in a different decade.

President Wilson wasn't fond of the tactics of Alice Paul and the National Woman's Party. But he understood that he needed to consider supporting a suffrage amendment because the movement was growing in both numbers and in political influence. He was also appalled that suffragists were tortured and force-fed at Occoquan Workhouse as American women were being asked to support their sons and husbands who were fighting World War I by this time. So, on September 30, 1918, Wilson addressed Congress and publicly announced his support for women's suffrage. "We have made partners of the women in this war," he said during his congressional address. "Shall we admit them only to a partnership of suffering and sacrifice and toil and not to a partnership of privilege and right?"

Despite Wilson's support, on February 10, 1919, the Senate failed to gather enough votes to pass the proposed Nineteenth Amendment, which would guarantee female suffrage. The National Woman's Party lobbied senators, disrupted the Republican National Convention, and burned copies of Wilson's speeches in front of the White House. Meanwhile, the NAWSA were still holding annual conventions and

THE NIGHT OF TERROR

When radical suffragists, including Alice Paul, were arrested for civil disobedience, they were given an option: Pay a fine or be sent to Occoquan Workhouse in Virginia. At first, the arrests were for "obstructing the sidewalk"; they came with three-day sentences and twenty-five-dollar fines.

Suffragists jailed in the workhouse were treated poorly and only fed bread and water. When Paul tried to initiate a hunger strike, she was force-fed. In an interview with the *Philadelphia Tribune*, Paul explained this torture: "When the forcible feeding was ordered I was taken from my bed, carried to another room, and forced into a chair, bound with sheets and sat upon bodily by a fat murderess, whose duty it was to keep me still. Then the prison doctor, assisted by two woman attendants, placed a rubber tube up my nostrils and pumped liquid food through it into the stomach."

The battle between police officers in Washington, DC, and suffragists reached a fever pitch on November 10, 1917. Thirty-three suffragists were lined up outside of the White House's wrought-iron fence with their protest signs. Toward the end of a long day of picketing, the protestors were swarmed by police and trotted off to the Occoquan Workhouse. Though the women were accustomed to facing some mistreatment, the guards in the Northern Virginian prison took their punishment to the next level at the behest of Superintendent W. H. Whittaker: Lucy Burns's hands were tied to a bar above her cell, and she was forced to stand up all night. Other suffragists were beaten up, their hands smashed against iron beds; one suffragist, Alice Cosu, had a heart attack, but was denied treatment until the next morning. "In the morning we were taken one by one to a washroom at the end of the hall," suffragist Dorothy Day wrote in her memoir, *The Long Loneliness*. "There was a toilet in each cell, open, and paper and flushing were supplied by the guard. It was as though one were in a zoo with the open bars leading into the corridor."

The protesters were released after two weeks, and by that time, the "night of terror" had become a crucial turning point in public opinion about the suffrage movement.

sticking to their strategy of a state-by-state lobbying approach. They also created a league of woman voters who focused solely on obtaining full suffrage for women. While Black women were still concerned with suffrage, they were mostly in their communities, continuing to work on bettering their neighborhood schools and other aspects of racial uplift.

After another year of protests and Wilson personally writing to individual senators to persuade them to pass the Nineteenth Amendment, the bill finally passed the House of Representatives on May 21, 1919, and the Senate on June 4, 1919. It took one last, hard-fought dramatic struggle— right down to one vote—for the Nineteenth Amendment to be fully ratified and added to the Constitution. On August 26, 1920, nearly twenty-six million American women at long last got the right to vote.

The earliest and most stalwart of suffragists did not live to see this happen. Black woman suffragists who'd fought to gain the right to vote died before they could ever cast a ballot. Mary Ann Shadd Cary, one of the only Black women to speak at the 1878 National Woman Suffrage Association conference, died in 1893 at the age of seventy. Frances Ellen Watkins Harper, a founding member of the American Woman Suffrage Association, died in 1911 at the age of eighty-five. Charlotte Forten Grimké died in 1914 at the age of seventy-six. Adella Hunt Logan died in 1915 at the age of fifty-two. The passage of the Nineteenth Amendment was bittersweet for the Black woman suffragists who were still alive, like Mary Church Terrell and Ida B. Wells-Barnett. Based on the racist, rights-blocking experiences of Black men who had had the right to vote since 1870, Black women knew the fight for full and free suffrage was far from over. They knew they'd have to turn all their energies toward ending segregation—and using their new voting power to elect officials who supported that cause.

Suffragist surrounded by newspaper clippings about the passage of the Nineteenth Amendment.

EIGHT

Voting Out Jim Crow

The war over suffrage was seemingly won in August 1920, when after more than seventy years of activism, Tennessee became the thirty-fifth and final state to ratify the Nineteenth Amendment, guaranteeing that it would become federal law. Four months later, when the first post–Nineteenth Amendment election was held on November 2, 1920, scores of newly registered female voters headed to the polls for the first time. There was a lot of renewed enthusiasm about voting rights among Black woman voters, who registered in droves in Northern states, including New York and Pennsylvania, and even in some Southern states. In 1920, there were more Black women than white women registered to vote in Florida, and Anna Simms Banks, a schoolteacher from Kentucky, was elected to be a delegate at the state's Congressional District Republican Convention. Delegates represent their district or county at a state convention where they cast a vote for the person who will represent their party in the national election, so Banks helped decide Kentucky's Republican presidential candidate for the 1920 election. There were eight million more votes cast in the 1920 election than in the 1916 election, which had a lot to do with the Nineteenth Amendment. Even with this new right, though, only 36 percent of eligible woman voters cast a ballot.

The ratification of the Nineteenth Amendment didn't solve the problems around voting for Black women, many of whom knew that Black men in their communities had been maimed, hung from trees, and run out of town for trying to vote. Legally, Black men were granted suffrage by the Fifteenth Amendment, but the majority of them were barred from voting and threatened with racial violence when they attempted to register to vote. The barriers around voting weren't going to magically disappear because women's suffrage was now enshrined in law. The reality was much more complicated for Black women, especially those who lived in Southern states.

Between 1890 and 1910, ten states, including Mississippi, Alabama, and Georgia, had passed laws that made it completely impossible to protect and enforce the voting rights that both Black men and women now had access to. In Louisiana, for instance, only 730 African Americans were registered to vote, though there were more Blacks in the state than whites. In 1901, when Alabama was drafting a new constitution, attorney John B. Knox, who presided over the state's Constitutional Convention, said that their aim was "to establish white supremacy in this state. If we should have white supremacy, we must establish it by law—not by force or fraud."

In the early twentieth century, more Americans could legally vote—but exercising that right was not guaranteed. The fight for the right to vote was really a part of a bigger struggle for dignity, for being seen as and treated as an equal citizen. For this reason, the act of voting was also tied closely to other elements of citizenship. For instance, only registered voters could run for local office or serve on juries. If voting rules excluded you from the voter rolls and made you ineligible to vote, you couldn't consider running for Congress or even going for a seat on a local school board or running for judge. Stripping Black people of their ability to vote was really about barring them from participating in every element of public life, just like segregating African Americans in separate schools, restaurants, bathrooms, trains, and even hospitals. Libraries, parks, schools, drinking fountains, buses, trains, restaurants, and stores posted "Whites Only" and "Colored" signs, which communicated to Black people where they could and couldn't go. These "Jim Crow" laws and restrictions were created in Southern states in the 1890s in order to separate white Americans from Black Americans and keep Black Americans from earning a decent wage, buying property, voting, and enjoying all the civic rights afforded to white Americans. Jim Crow laws also kept African Americans from even attempting to register to vote in many places. They knew there was a good chance they'd be denied—or even met with violence.

Educator Mary McLeod Bethune was still running her overcrowded four-story school for Black girls in Daytona Beach, Florida, when the Nineteenth Amendment passed. Bethune felt revitalized by its ratification. It gave her a renewed purpose beyond running a school that didn't always have the resources it needed. The state of Florida, however, was less than thrilled that both Black men and Black women now had the legal right to vote. In 1885, fifteen years after the Fifteenth Amendment was ratified, the state had imposed a "poll tax" that required Black voters to pay a set amount of money before they were allowed to register. Black voters who were accused of committing crimes were also immediately removed from voter-registration rolls. So, after the passage of the Nineteenth Amendment, Bethune began focusing on helping Black voters get around those obstacles.

Bethune once again hit the streets, biking through Daytona's neighborhoods and knocking on doors. This time, she was asking for donations to help Black voters pay poll taxes so that more people could afford to register. Bethune also opened the doors of the Daytona Normal and Industrial Institute to tutor Black people who needed help studying for the literacy test that was given to them when they tried to register to vote. Night in and night out, no matter how tired she was, Bethune tutored children and adults alike, and in her free time, she planned a mass registration drive where she'd lead all the adults she was tutoring from her school to a clerk's office to get them registered to vote.

Bethune's activism soon caught the attention of the white supremacist terrorist group the Ku Klux Klan. Members of the local KKK chapter and other white bigots wreaked havoc in Florida. Between 1877 and 1950, more than 330 Black people were lynched in the state; in 1920, racial tensions were reaching a fever pitch, thanks to the passage of the Nineteenth Amendment. So Bethune wasn't alarmed or even surprised when she learned that white supremacists were threatening to burn down her school. She remained calm. After teaching her night class and sending many of her students home, she, her groundskeeper, and some students whom she asked to remain behind stood vigil outside of the school and looked out for KKK members. The Klan never showed, and the very next day, Bethune led more than one hundred Black people to the polls to register to vote and cast their very first ballots in Daytona's mayoral race. Staring down the KKK and following through with the march to vote turned Bethune into a local celebrity, which brought an influx of money and other resources to the school. In turn, she opened Daytona Normal and Industrial Institute's library to the public, making it the state's first free library for African Americans.

Outside of her work in the Daytona community, Bethune was still actively involved in the National Association of Colored Women's Clubs, which now had more than ten thousand members throughout the United States. After the passage of the Nineteenth Amendment, the NACWC continued helping Black women "improve their own condition and that of their race" by investing in community programs, such as schools in Virginia and Savannah, Georgia; Black-owned and -operated hospitals in New York and Mississippi; nurseries and free kindergarten programs in Chicago, Illinois, and Oakland, California; and foster homes for "delinquent" girls in Arkansas and Atlanta, Georgia. For members of the NACWC, suffrage was just one part of improving the "conditions for family living." The organization's leaders, including President Hallie Q. Brown, were "especially interested in the problems of women of color who had the added disadvantage of race and economic state." So, though their programs didn't directly relate to voting rights, these schools, hospitals, and homes helped improve their communities. The NACWC's approach to bettering Black communities really appealed to Bethune, who was doing exactly that in her own neighborhood. When the Republican National Committee asked Hallie Q. Brown to leave the NACWC and come lead their party's efforts to reach Black woman voters, Bethune decided to run to become the organization's next president.

The NACWC's members descended on Chicago, Illinois, in 1924 for the organization's fourteenth annual convention. Bethune was ready to persuade them to vote for her to be their next president. However, she had some stiff competition: Ida B. Wells-Barnett, who still called Chicago home and had spent the past four years running the Alpha Suffrage Club, also wanted to be president of the NACWC. She'd become really interested in both running a national organization, since the Alpha Suffrage Club focused its efforts on Chicago, and running for office, after she'd helped elect Oscar DePriest as the city's first African American alderman.

Two powerhouses running against each other raised some eyebrows, but Bethune and Wells-Barnett were cordial to each other during the convention proceedings. When Bethune won the election, becoming the NACWC's seventh president, Wells-Barnett continued supporting her and the organization.

As president of the NACWC, Bethune inherited an organization that didn't have enough money to cover its expenses. The NACWC didn't have a national headquarters; there wasn't a secretary to keep records of meetings or conventions; and there wasn't a national list of donors whom Bethune could contact to ask for money. When Bethune realized how dire the situation was for the NACWC, she made the difficult decision to leave Florida, move to Washington, DC, and focus full time on fundraising for the organization. But there was still a big problem with her plan: She had a school in Daytona Beach, Florida, to look after, and she didn't want to abandon her students, especially where there were so few schools for Black children in the area.

Bethune returned to Florida and traveled to Jacksonville, a city about an hour away from Daytona Beach, to meet with Reverend S. B. Darnell, the founder and principal of the Cookman Institute, an elementary and high school that educated Jacksonville's Black community. In 1923, they'd started talking about merging their schools, but Bethune felt hesitant to turn her all-girls school into a coed institution. When Bethune returned to Jacksonville, however, her need was more urgent, so she and Darnell came to an agreement: Their schools would become the Daytona-Cookman Collegiate Institute, a coed college, and they'd become a part of the United Methodist Church. With this agreement squared away, Bethune became the president of the Daytona-Cookman Collegiate Institute, a role that allowed her to still be involved without needing to be in Daytona Beach all the time.

Bethune returned to Washington, DC, and became part of a community of other prominent Black and white women who were also working to improve the lives of Black people throughout the United States and protect their right to vote. Bethune was the only Black attendee at a 1927 luncheon in New York hosted by Eleanor Roosevelt, wife of then New York State Governor Franklin Delano Roosevelt; they became fast friends. Roosevelt, who called Bethune "her closest friend in her age group," introduced Bethune to wider circles where white politicians, including President Calvin Coolidge, requested her counsel about how to reach Black voters. By then, Mary Church Terrell, the first president of the NACWC, who once predicted that Bethune would become the organization's president, was presiding over the Republican

Women's League, a subset of the Republican National Committee that helped register woman and African American voters and support woman candidates. After her husband died in 1925, Terrell threw herself further into her work with the Republican National Committee, even helping activist Ruth Hannah McCormick successfully run for a House of Representatives seat in Illinois in 1928. However, Terrell, who was sixty-five, Bethune, who was fifty, and Wells-Barnett, who was sixty-three, recognized that they needed to begin grooming other Black woman leaders in Chicago, Washington, DC, and beyond to carry on their activism after they were gone. Unfortunately, all their efforts came to a halt when the US economy crashed in 1929, sending all Americans, especially Black Americans, into a tailspin.

When the Great Depression hit, 38 percent of Black Americans

Mary McLeod Bethun, left, and Eleanor Roosevelt, who became close friends, at the opening of Midway Hall in Washington, DC, in May 1943.

could no longer afford to feed their families without assistance from the government. Black women, many of whom worked as teachers and domestic servants to support their families, began losing their jobs in droves to white men who needed jobs to stay afloat. Black women were pushed out of the labor force as unemployment rates reached an all-time high for Black people, leading the National Association for the Advancement of Colored People to prioritize finding jobs for Black men.

Though Wells-Barnett unsuccessfully tried to run for the Illinois State Senate in 1930, most esteemed Black suffragists were now more concerned with helping their communities survive than with fighting for voting rights. When Franklin Delano Roosevelt became president of the United States in 1933, America's economy was still in free fall. Roosevelt came from an affluent New York family and community. He couldn't fully grasp the impact of the Great Depression on Black Americans. Eleanor Roosevelt knew exactly who could help her husband understand the racial dynamics of the recession.

Eleanor Roosevelt called Mary McLeod Bethune, who was still splitting her time between Daytona Beach, Florida, and Washington, DC. The first lady asked her to move to DC permanently and become President Roosevelt's special advisor on minority affairs and a member of the National Youth Administration, a new initiative that would educate young Americans and then help them find jobs. Bethune, who had become disenchanted with the National Association of Colored Women's Clubs because their members spent so much time lobbying for bills instead of helping Black people "learn the simples of farming, making decent homes, of health and plain cleanliness," agreed. Moving to DC on a full-time

VOTE FOR

☒ **Mrs. Ida B. Wells-Barnett**
3624 So. Parkway

CANDIDATE FOR

DELEGATE

To Republican Nat'l Convention

AT KANSAS CITY, MO.

JUNE 1928

PRIMARY TUESDAY, APRIL 10

In 1928, Ida B. Wells-Barnett ran a campaign to be one of the Republican Party's delegates for the Republican National Convention, taking place in Kansas City, Missouri, in June. She later ran as an independent for the Illinois State Senate, but her bid was unsuccessful.

basis would allow her to work on the germ of an idea that she'd been thinking about for a long time, mainly taking what she'd learned at the NACWC and applying it to a new organization that would specifically focus on ending discrimination.

On December 5, 1935, Bethune created the National Council of Negro Women (NCNW), an organization that consisted of twenty-eight groups, including the American Federation of Teachers and Delta Sigma Theta Sorority, Inc., coming together as champions for Black women's rights, including fighting poverty, passing anti-lynching bills, preserving voting rights, and ending discrimination in employment so that more Black women could find jobs. Bethune was committed to developing "competent and courageous leadership among negro women," so the NCNW, which would later include a number of influential Black women, quickly outlined a set of priorities in their magazine, *African Woman's Journal*, including outlawing the poll tax, ending segregation in the military, and demanding that

Black history be taught in all public schools. The NCNW soon became a force, much to the delight of both Bethune and Eleanor Roosevelt. Both women were pushing hard to make sure there were more Black people represented in President Roosevelt's cabinet as he and his advisors rolled out the New Deal, a number of laws, reforms, and projects that the president hoped would reverse the economic recession. By the time the NCNW was founded, there were forty-five Black people working as a part of the Federal Council of Negro Affairs, which Bethune jokingly called the "Black Cabinet," and she was the highest-ranking Black woman in the federal government. "We have had a chance to look down the stream of the forty-eight states and evaluate the type of work and positions secured by Negroes," Bethune said about the "Black Cabinet." "The responsibility rests on us. Let us band together and work together as one big brotherhood and give momentum to the

This photo, taken on April 21, 1945, showcases members of the National Council of Negro Women entertaining British war workers and white American women who'd toured Great Britain for eight weeks.

great ball that is starting to roll for Negroes." Still, Bethune could feel all the weight of the activism she'd been doing for more than thirty years, so she continued scouring for other Black women who could eventually take the baton. Ida B. Wells-Barnett had died in 1931, so the issue was even more urgent for Bethune, who realized that she was also getting older.

Bethune's relationship with Roosevelt brought her closer to some budding Black woman activists, including Dorothy Irene Height, an educator and activist from Rankin, Pennsylvania, who'd taught at Brooklyn, New York's Brownsville Community Center and was now working at a YMCA in Harlem, New York. That meeting changed the trajectory of Height's life, as she later wrote in her autobiography: "She drew me into her dazzling orbit of people in power and people in poverty. I remember how she made her fingers into a fist to illustrate for the women the significance of working together to eliminate injustice. 'The freedom gates are half ajar,' she said. 'We must pry them fully open.'"

Within a year of meeting Bethune at a speech Eleanor Roosevelt gave at the Harlem YMCA in fall 1937, Height was promoted to executive director of the YWCA's Phyllis Wheatley Association in Washington, DC. She turned her focus toward desegregation, an issue that still plagued Black people throughout the United States. The YWCA was still segregated into "Whites Only" and "Coloreds Only" branches when Height joined the national leadership team, and she worked to end that, ensuring that all YWCA branches were integrated. Her work on segregation reflected the NCNW's work on the same issue in many other areas, especially in the military.

At that time, Black men who volunteered for duty or were drafted into the armed forces were immediately sent to all-Black units where they mostly worked in supporting roles rather than being on the front lines. Similarly, the Army Nurse Corps, one of the few branches of the military that accepted women, only admitted white nurses, which greatly disappointed Mary McLeod Bethune, who'd opened a hospital in Daytona Beach, Florida, that hired Black nurses and doctors and treated Black patients. When Bethune learned that the military planned to continue segregating troops as the United States geared up for World War II, she enlisted Height and other members of the NCNW to help lobby President Roosevelt to desegregate the armed forces. The NCNW joined the US War Department's Bureau of Public Relations, where they were able to persuade President Roosevelt to admit Black women into the army and start desegregating divisions. Though Southern states still remained resistant to integration, World War II demanded more troops, so eventually the military was ordered to fully integrate. It was an important victory that set the stage for other elements of American life to begin integrating, including schools.

"I feel a sense of peace," Bethune said in 1949 when she decided to retire as president of the NCNW. "Women united around the National Council of Negro Women, have made purposeful strides in the march toward democratic living. They have moved mountains." Her decision to bow out from the organization she'd created marked a turn for woman suffragists. It was the ending of an era and the beginning of another, one focused primarily on gaining civil rights, including voting, for Black people.

In 1954, the Supreme Court ruled in *Brown v. Board of Education*

Dorothy Irene Height (1912–2010) presents Eleanor Roosevelt with the Mary McLeod Bethune Human Rights Award on November 12, 1960. Height's mother had been actively involved in the Pennsylvania Federation of Colored Women's Clubs, and brought her young daughter to every meeting. "There I saw women working, organizing, teaching themselves," Height once said. "Since those early days, I've never doubted my place in the sisterhood." Height became an heir to Bethune's legacy, joining the National Council of Negro Women and becoming one of the YWCA's national leaders.

that it was illegal to segregate Black and white students in separate schools. By this time, the old guard, including Mary Church Terrell and Mary McLeod Bethune, had died or retired from activism. But other Black woman activists were ready to carry on their work.

In 1957, Dorothy Irene Height became the president of the National Council of Negro Women, and she turned the organization's focus toward the next phase of what was becoming the Civil Rights Movement: integrating housing and securing the right to vote. Height was the only woman invited to be on the administrative committee for the August 28, 1963, March on Washington for Jobs and Freedom, where Reverend Dr. Martin Luther King Jr. gave his iconic "I Have a Dream" speech.

Though King's wife, Coretta Scott King, was a member of the NCNW and said she'd "long admired this organization, its great work, and its noble purposes," the March on Washington's organizers refused to allow women to speak, which disappointed Height. "I've never seen a more immovable force. We could not get women's participation taken seriously." She wasn't allowed to deliver a speech, but Height's mere presence signaled her influence as the head of the NCNW. After the March on Washington, she and other women "became much more aware and much more aggressive in facing up to sexism in our dealings with the male leadership in the movement." Much like the original suffrage movement, the Civil Rights Movement sidelined Black women, relegating them to the background even as they contributed so much to the fight for civil rights.

In 1964, President Lyndon B. Johnson signed the Civil Rights Act. It was supposed to end segregation in public places and stop employment discrimination on the basis of race, color, religion, sex, or national origin. It also briefly touched on voting. The Civil Rights Act of 1964 mandated that if there were literacy tests, they had to be given to every voter, not just Black voters; it also said that all people, regardless of education level, could vote.

After the passage of the Civil Rights Act, two of the most important civil rights organizations—the Southern Christian Leadership Conference (SCLC), led by Martin Luther King Jr., and the Student Nonviolent Coordinating Committee (SNCC)—turned their attention toward helping Black people register to vote, and so did the women who were a part of those organizations. Fannie Lou Hamer, a sharecropper from Mississippi, was one of them.

Hamer was "sick and tired of feeling sick and tired" after experiencing racism throughout her entire life. In the 1950s, when she was in her late thirties, she became interested in the Civil Rights Movement after attending meetings at the Regional Council of Negro Leadership (RCNL), a local civil rights organization that was working hard to convince people in Mississippi to register to vote. At the time, less than 2 percent of African Americans in Mississippi were registered to vote because of poll taxes, literacy tests, and other hurdles that kept them from exercising their rights.

"I didn't know anything about registering to vote," Hamer explained later. "One night I went to the church. They had a mass meeting. . . . They talked about how it was our right, that we could register and vote." Hamer was the first person at the RCNL meeting to volunteer to travel to Indianola, Mississippi, to register to vote.

On a hot summer morning on August 31, 1962, Hamer boarded a bus alongside eighteen other RCNL members to start the long trip to Indianola. As the bus bounced over country roads, Hamer sang hymns, such as "Go Tell It on the Mountain" and "This Little Light of Mine," to calm herself and the other passengers.

The first time Fannie Lou Hamer (1917–1977) tried to register to vote, an administrator made her copy Mississippi's state constitution down word for word, explain what each section of the constitution meant, and then asked her to explain what a "de facto law" is. Hamer responded, "I knowed as much about a facto law as a horse knows about Christmas Day." There is no such thing as a "de facto law," but these kinds of trick questions were often used to disqualify Black people from registering to vote.

When Hamer and her church group boarded the bus to return to Sunflower County, none of them had succeeded in registering to vote because of all the hurdles the officials put them through. But she still faced repercussions for even trying. When the person who owned the sharecropping land that Hamer's family lived and worked on learned that she'd tried to register to vote, he told Hamer, "You'll have to go down and withdraw your registration, or you'll have to leave this place." A month after being denied the right to vote, Hamer was standing in her yard when a group of white men drove quickly toward her house. They opened fire, shooting at Hamer and her husband more than sixteen times before quickly speeding off. No one was harmed, but Hamer and her family were still shaken up, so they decided to relocate to Tallahatchie County, Mississippi.

After Hamer passed the literacy test on January 10, 1963, and officially became a registered voter in Mississippi, she learned that she couldn't vote until she paid the poll tax. It was just another barrier erected to keep Black people from exercising their political power, and Hamer knew it. Meanwhile, Hamer's fearlessness attracted the attention of Bob Moses, an SNCC organizer. Moses told another organizer to find "the lady who sings the hymns," and he recruited her to help SNCC register voters. She began traveling throughout the South with other SNCC organizers. It was a dangerous mission.

On June 9, 1963, Hamer and other SNCC organizers were traveling from Charleston, South Carolina, to Greenwood, Mississippi, when they were arrested on false charges. Once they were in jail, Hamer and other activists were brutally beaten by police officers. Hamer was beaten with a blackjack by two inmates at the request of police officers, and when she tried to fight, an officer "walked over, took my dress, pulled it up over my shoulders, leaving my body exposed to five men." She was beaten so badly that her kidneys were permanently damaged, and she developed a blood clot in her left eye.

The kind of violence that Hamer experienced was common for African American organizers trying to get out the vote across the

South, as Ella Baker, a civil rights activist who worked for both the SCLC and SNCC, knew all too well.

Baker, who attended segregated schools in North Carolina before moving to New York City to work as a secretary for the NAACP, was integral to helping Dr. King and other civil rights leaders register voters. She organized the SCLC's Crusade for Citizenship, a voter registration campaign that nearly doubled the number of Black voters ahead of the 1958 and 1960 elections. She was also a founding member of SNCC, and helped the organization orchestrate its Freedom Summer, or Mississippi Summer Project, a seminal three-month registration drive that began in June 1964. At that time, 6 percent of Mississippi's eligible Black voters were registered; volunteers were in the state to increase that percentage.

Southern newspapers bashed Freedom Summer volunteers as "unshaven and unwanted trash." They were frequently exposed to beatings, intimidation, and harassment that not only impacted the volunteers, but also the people they were attempting to register. Over the course of ten weeks of Freedom Summer, more than one thousand people were arrested and thirty homes that belonged to African Americans were bombed or burned to the ground. And most egregiously, three volunteers—James

Ella Baker (1903–1986) is often called the Mother of the Civil Rights Movement. This photo was taken by noted Civil Rights Movement photographer Danny Lyon in 1946.

Chaney, Andrew Goodman, and Michael Schwerner—were kidnapped and murdered by members of the Ku Klux Klan. Despite the traumatic experiences that Freedom Summer volunteers experienced, they were still committed to registering voters in Mississippi and helping them exercise their right to vote.

Fannie Lou Hamer wanted to take it one step further. She worked with SNCC to create the Mississippi Freedom Democratic Party (MFDP) or "Freedom Democrats" in the summer of 1964. They intended to go to the Democratic National Convention in Atlantic City, New Jersey, and cast a vote to determine the party's next presidential candidate. Hamer also planned to run for Congress against an incumbent who had already been elected to office twelve times. In a magazine interview, Hamer explained, "I'm showing the people that a Negro can run for office."

At the Democratic National Convention, the Mississippi Freedom Democratic Party wanted to challenge the all-white delegation that was representing their state. But instead, Hamer was invited by the Democratic National Convention's Credentials Committee to testify in front of Congress about all the obstacles she'd encountered as she tried to register to vote and register other voters. In a "deep, powerful voice" that "shakes the air," Hamer recounted the horrific night she spent in that Mississippi jail. "All of this is on account of we want to register, to become first-class citizens," she said at the end of her powerful speech. "And if the Freedom Democratic Party is not seated now, I question America. Is this America, the land of the free and the home of the brave, where we have to sleep with our telephones off the hooks because our lives be threatened daily, because we want to live as decent human beings, in America?"

Hamer's speech resounded in the chamber, which remained dead silent as those present hung on her every word. However, President Lyndon B. Johnson, who had assumed the presidency after the assassination of John F. Kennedy, was concerned that her speech would overshadow the entire convention, so he planned an impromptu press conference at the same time as her testimony. This prevented Hamer's speech from being broadcast on television, but later that evening, all the newscasts aired it.

Johnson was greatly opposed to seating Freedom Democrats in the Mississippi delegation, but he also knew that not supporting civil rights could cost him some votes in the North. So Johnson met with Senator Hubert Humphrey, who was vying for the vice presidential nomination, and a few others, and created a compromise: They would give the Freedom Democrats two nonvoting seats on the Mississippi delegation in exchange for their endorsement. Hamer was incredibly offended by this offer, and she expressed as much directly to Humphrey. "Do you mean to tell me that your position is more important than four hundred thousand Black people's lives? Senator Humphrey, I know lots of people in Mississippi who have lost their jobs trying to register to vote. I had to leave the plantation where I worked in Sunflower County, Mississippi. Now if you lose this job of Vice-President because you do what is right, because you help the MFDP, everything will be all right. God will take care of you. . . . But if you take [the nomination] this way, why, you will never be able to do any good for civil rights, for poor people, for peace, or any of those things you talk about." Ultimately, the Freedom Democrats rejected Johnson's offer and didn't help elect the party's candidate.

Meanwhile, Ella Baker and the SCLC were also taking direct action to register voters in Alabama. Only a very small percentage of Black residents in Alabama were registered to vote for many of the same reasons that stopped African Americans in Mississippi from registering. Poll taxes, threats of violence, and literacy tests were keeping many Black people in Alabama from voting, but Dr. King, Ella Baker, and the SCLC had a plan to break that wide open.

Selma, Alabama, was historically resistant to African Americans registering to vote because their county sheriff, Jim Clark, would personally block the entrance to the county courthouse and beat and arrest Black voters who attempted to register. He'd punched Annie Lee Cooper, a Black woman trying to register, in the face because she'd refused to leave after standing for hours, waiting to vote. He'd also arrested three hundred students who were silently protesting outside of the courthouse, and then made them walk more than three miles to jail. Clark was notorious, and his actions made it impossible for Selma's Black residents to vote. Only three hundred of the city's fifteen thousand Black residents were registered.

So Dr. King, Ella Baker, and other members of the SCLC started spreading the word: On March 7, 1965, they and members of the Black community would dress in their best clothes—suits and ties, dresses that were suitable for church, and professional shoes—and walk fifty-four miles from Selma to Montgomery, the capital of Alabama. More than six hundred marchers gathered in Selma on March 7; they started walking toward US Route 80, the highway that would get them all the way to Montgomery. About six blocks into the march, as they approached the Edmund Pettus Bridge, a number of state troopers and white residents of Selma attacked them, hitting them with billy clubs, spraying them with tear gas, and leaving

AMELIA BOYNTON ROBINSON

Amelia (Platts) Boynton Robinson (1911–2015), was a central figure in the Civil Rights Movement. As a child raised in Savannah, Georgia, Robinson was interested in women's suffrage. She often climbed into a horse and buggy with her mother and drove around their community passing out suffrage pamphlets to their neighbors. It was Robinson's first taste of activism, and that passion remained with her for the rest of her life.

Robinson graduated from Tuskegee Institute—now known as Tuskegee University—with a home economics degree in 1927, and then moved to Selma, Alabama, where she worked at the US Department of Agriculture.

Though it was difficult to register to vote in Selma in the 1930s, Robinson refused to be turned away, and in 1934, she became one of the only Black residents in the city to become a registered voter. Thirty years later, in 1964, Robinson became the first woman to run for Congress in Alabama. Though she only won 10 percent of the vote, her insider knowledge of Selma's politics made her a valuable part of the Southern Christian Leadership Conference's plan to organize the march from Selma to Montgomery on March 7, 1965. During the march, Robinson was brutally beaten unconscious and teargassed, and a photo of her lying bloody on the ground was plastered in newspapers all around the world. She had to be carried away after the march was over.

In a 2014 interview, conducted one year before she died, Robinson described what happened. "Then they charged. They came from the right. They came from the left. One [of the troopers] shouted: 'Run!' I thought, 'Why should I be running?' Then an officer on horseback hit me across the back of the shoulders and, for a second time, on the back of the neck. I lost consciousness."

Though Robinson felt the effects of the tear gas for many years and said that "it could have killed me," she also said, "It made me more determined to do everything I could to make African Americans first-class citizens and to destroy the fear that is in our people." Robinson's activism and sacrifices were depicted in director Ava DuVernay's Oscar-nominated film *Selma*.

many of the marchers unconscious. The event, which became known as Bloody Sunday, became a major turning point in the fight for a federal voting rights act. The entire confrontation was captured through news photographs and by television cameras, and broadcast throughout the country and internationally; many Americans were outraged by what they saw.

Two days later, Dr. King and other protesters returned to the Edmund Pettus Bridge to initiate another march, but they didn't have the proper clearance, so they decided not to march that day. However, the SCLC's goal had been accomplished. President Johnson saw the horrors that were being inflicted on African Americans who were simply trying to register to vote, and he made the decision to appeal to Congress to pass the Voting Rights Act.

On March 15, 1965, President Johnson arrived at the House of Representatives at 9:02 p.m. and delivered a speech that shook America to its core. "There is no cause for pride in what has happened in Selma. There is no cause for self-satisfaction in the long denial of equal rights of millions of Americans. But there is cause for hope and for faith in our democracy in what is happening here tonight," he began. "For the cries of pain and the hymns and protests of oppressed people have summoned into convocation all the majesty of this great Government—the Government of the greatest Nation on earth. Our mission is at once the oldest and the most basic of this country: to right wrong, to do justice, to serve man."

Johnson had drafted a bill that would "eliminate illegal barriers to the right to vote," and urged both Democrats and Republicans to review it and vote on it as quickly as possible. "There is no constitutional issue here. The command of the Constitution is plain," he said toward the end of the speech. "There is no moral issue. It is wrong—deadly wrong—to deny any of your fellow Americans the right to vote in this country. There is no issue of States rights or national rights. There is only the struggle for human rights." The Voting Rights Act of 1965 was introduced in the House of Representatives on March 17, 1965, and introduced in the Senate on March 19, 1965.

While Congress debated the provisions of the bill, the SCLC was preparing to stage another march from Selma to Montgomery on March 21, but they were rightfully concerned about their safety. On Wednesday, March 17, President Johnson agreed to send federal troops to Selma and Montgomery to protect the marchers, and federal district court judge Frank Minis Johnson granted them permission to hold the march, based on their First Amendment rights. This time, nearly eight thousand people gathered to start the trek from Selma to Montgomery, and on March 25, more than twenty-five thousand people gathered in Montgomery to cheer on the protesters, who'd walked through freezing rain to get there.

After the successful march, Ella Baker, Fannie Lou Hamer, and the other Black women who were fighting for voting rights waited with bated breath to learn the fate of the Voting Rights Act. They breathed a sigh of relief on May 26 when the Senate passed the bill, and on July 9 when it passed the US House of Representatives. The Voting Rights Act was officially signed into law by President Johnson on August 6, with Dr. King, Amelia Boynton Robinson, and other movement leaders surrounding him. More than forty-five years after white women were granted suffrage, Black women now finally had the real and actual right to vote, but so many of them didn't live to see all their hard work crystallized in law.

On August 6, 1965, President Lyndon B. Johnson signed the Voting Rights Act of 1965. He was surrounded by Civil Rights Movement leaders, including Reverend Dr. Martin Luther King Jr.

Nannie Helen Burroughs, Ida B. Wells-Barnett, Anna Julia Cooper, and a number of other Black woman suffragists died before they were able to cast their ballots without any obstacles, making the victory even more bittersweet. However, after President Johnson signed the Voting Rights Act into law, there was an immediately positive impact on Black voters in Southern states where they'd previously been

beaten up and threatened for even attempting to register. In Mississippi, the voter registration percentage jumped from 6.7 percent in 1965 to 59.8 percent in 1967. In order to achieve this, the Voting Rights Act included key provisions: Section 4 established a formula to identify counties and cities that had barriers in place for Black voters, including a five-year suspension of "tests or devices," like poll taxes and literacy tests, that kept Black people from the ballot box. These counties and cities were closely monitored by the federal government, and if they wanted to incorporate any changes to their voting laws, it had to be approved either by the United States District Court for the District of Columbia or by the attorney general. The goal of the Voting Rights Act was to eliminate barriers to voting, and for forty-eight years, it was successful.

During those years, both Fannie Lou Hamer and Amelia Boynton Robinson ran for Congress, though neither woman's campaign was successful. Still, in 1968, just three years after the VRA, Shirley Chisholm of New York became the first Black woman elected to Congress. That could not have happened without the passage of the Voting Rights Act. The VRA was reauthorized in 1970 for five years,

Shirley Chisholm (1924–2005) of New York was the first Black woman elected to Congress. In 1972, she became the first African American to run for president of the United States. Her powerful campaign slogan was "unbought and unbossed."

in 1975 for seven years, and in 1982 for twenty-five years. In 2006, the formula to determine whether or not counties or cities were in compliance with the VRA was extended again for twenty-five years. In 1970 and 1975, the Supreme Court also extended the Voting Rights Act's protection to include voting discrimination against people of "language minority groups," or voters who didn't speak English as a first language.

It seemed that there was a general consensus about the importance and necessity of the Voting Rights Act, especially after Barack Obama, the first Black president, was elected in 2008. However, after the 2010 midterm elections led to a number of state legislatures and governors flipping from Democratic to Republican control, a deluge of laws were passed to restrict voting in multiple states. As the editorial board of the *New York Times* stated in 2015, "Today there are no poll taxes or literacy tests. Instead there are strict and unnecessary voter-identification requirements, or cutbacks to early voting and same-day registration—all of which are known to disproportionately burden Black voters."

One of the first ways that newly elected officials began dismantling the Voting Rights Act, starting around 2010, was to institute voter

ID laws. Essentially, these laws, which are currently on the books in thirty-four states, require voters to present an ID before they're allowed to cast a ballot. In seven states, including North Carolina, the law goes a little further by requiring voters to show specific forms of government-issued photo IDs in order to participate in the voting process. But voter ID laws are also really effective barriers: A 2014 study found that they reduce turnout by between 2 and 3 percentage points, which can translate into losing thousands of votes. Though many legislators claim that voter ID laws are designed to stop voter fraud—people voting when they are not eligible—that's not a real problem. A study found that between 2000 and 2014, a time period during which one billion ballots were cast, only thirty-one people have been found guilty of committing voter fraud. Despite the decades of suffrage work, in the twenty-first century, it is now harder to vote than ever for many people of color.

A 2011 protest march in New York City about preserving voting rights.

EPILOGUE

Continuing to Climb

When President Lyndon B. Johnson signed the Voting Rights Act into law in 1965, it included Sections 4 and 5, provisions that required cities, counties, and states with a history of racially discriminating against voters to get "preclearance" from either the United States Attorney General or a panel of judges in the United States District Court for the District of Columbia before they could make changes to their voting laws. Cities and counties governed by Sections 4 and 5 had to prove that their suggested rule or law change wouldn't "deny or abridge the right to vote on account of race, color, or membership in a language minority group" before it could be enacted. For more than four decades, Sections 4 and 5 remained intact, wielded against cities, counties, and entire states, including Alabama, North Carolina, South Carolina, Georgia, and Texas, where poll taxes, literacy tests, and racial violence once reigned supreme. Though the Voting Rights Act is considered one of the hallmarks of the Civil Rights Movement, which also included the passage of the Civil Rights Act of 1964 and the Civil Rights Act of 1968, Sections 4 and 5 have long been considered the "heart of the Voting Rights Act." These provisions were the sole parts of the VRA that guaranteed that racial discrimination in voting would be kept at bay.

The Voting Rights Act of 1965 came to a screeching halt on June 25, 2013, when the US Supreme Court struck down Section 4 as unconstitutional because it was based on "decades-old data and eradicated practices" that were unfair to states, cities, and counties— like Shelby County, Alabama, the one that brought the case to the Supreme Court—where "there is no longer such a disparity" between registered white and Black voters. Supreme Court Chief Justice John Roberts made this plain in his opinion about the court's decision:

> The formula captures States by reference to literacy tests and low voter registration and turnout in the 1960s and early 1970s. But such tests have been banned nationwide for over 40 years. And voter registration and turnout numbers in the covered States have risen dramatically in the years since. Racial disparity in those numbers was compelling evidence justifying the preclearance remedy and the coverage formula. There is no longer such a disparity.

Other Supreme Court justices, such as Ruth Bader Ginsburg, disagreed with the ruling. She wrote in her dissent that "throwing out preclearance when it has worked and is continuing to work is like throwing away your umbrella in a rainstorm because you are not getting wet." Alabama, Alaska, Arizona, Georgia, Louisiana, Mississippi, South Carolina, Texas, and Virginia were all freed from having to get preclearance before passing new voting rules and laws; the Supreme Court passed it back to Congress to draft a new formula to determine how cities, counties, and states would be monitored by the Voting Rights Act. As of this writing, Congress still hasn't done this.

Gutting the VRA ushered in a new and especially hard-hitting wave of voter suppression, much like what previous generations of Black suffragists faced. Within twenty-four hours, Texas introduced a bill that would require all potential voters to adhere to a strict ID policy, and that would immediately disqualify more than six hundred thousand voters in the state from casting a ballot. North Carolina, Alabama, and Georgia quickly followed suit. These states and others also began purging registered voters from their rolls, nixing same-day voter registration, closing polling places in predominantly Black communities, and employing a number of tactics to prevent Black voters and other voters of color from being able to exercise their rights. More than eight hundred polling locations had been closed across the country by the time of the 2016 presidential election. More than twenty-three states have passed laws that make it more difficult for people of color to vote. So, more than 171 years after the Seneca Falls Convention, Black people "continue to suffer significant, and profoundly unequal, limitations on their ability to vote."

Just as Sojourner Truth, Anna Julia Cooper, Mary McLeod Bethune, Fannie Lou Hamer, and so many others rose to the occasion, a new generation of suffragists are fighting to protect voting rights for Black people and people of color.

On March 7, 2015, political leaders commemorated the 50-year anniversary of Bloody Sunday with a march across the Edmund Pettus Bridge in Selma, Alabama. This photo includes then President Barack Obama and First Lady Michelle Obama; their children, Malia and Sasha; Amelia Boynton Robinson; and Representative John Lewis, who participated in the original march.

In November 2018, Georgia state representative Stacey Abrams lost a governorship race to Georgia secretary of state Brian Kemp. If she'd won, she would've been America's first Black woman governor, but instead, the historic election was mired in controversy about voting rights. Brian Kemp, as secretary of state, decided the state's voting laws, and as he ran against Abrams, he kept fifty-three thousand applications from new voters from being approved. Nearly 70 percent of those new voters were Black, a part of a long pattern of voters in Georgia being purged from rolls and denied the right to vote. From 2012 to 2016, 1.5 million voters were removed from Georgia's voter rolls. This rightfully alarmed Abrams, who said, "Voter suppression isn't only about blocking the vote. It is also about creating an atmosphere of fear, making sure their votes

An unnamed Black girl sits atop an adult's shoulder at the 50th anniversary commemoration of Bloody Sunday in Selma, Alabama, as Representative Lewis delivers a speech.

won't count." After Abrams narrowly lost the election to Kemp, she founded Fair Fight Action, an organization that's dedicated to making voting accessible to all Americans and to restoring Section 4 of the Voting Rights Act. "Voter suppression happens in every election, in every state. I need you all to talk about voter suppression all the time," Abrams has said. "We need to talk about voter suppression the way we talk about the Kardashians . . . with such insistence that people have to respond."

Restoring voting rights is critical as we approach a time when the majority of Americans will be people of color. It is estimated that there will be more people of color than white people in the United States by 2045, so guaranteeing that all people can exercise their right to vote is one of the only ways to ensure that equality continues being a part of America's future. The battle for voting rights will—and should—continue long after all the celebrations of the centennial of the Nineteenth Amendment. It is one of the most pressing issues of our time. Continuing to lift as we climb—by registering to vote, encouraging friends to register to vote, contacting congressional and state representatives to demand they take steps to protect voting rights, and keeping the universal suffrage conversation going—is essential. Voting is a hallmark of being an American citizen, and preserving the right to vote still matters—forever and always.

Bibliography

"Alice Paul Talks." *Philadelphia Tribune*. Philadelphia, 1910, https://www.loc.gov/resource/rbcmil.scrp6014202/?st=text.

Alonso, Harriet Hyman. *Peace as a Women's Issue: A History of the U.S. Movement for World Peace and Women's Rights*. Syracuse, N.Y.: Syracuse University Press, 1993.

Ansah, Ama. "Votes for Women means Votes for Black Women." National Women's History Museum. Accessed March 11, 2019, https://www.womenshistory.org/articles/votes-women-means-votes-black-women.

Anthony, Susan B. "Susan B. Anthony's Return to the 'Old Union' speech, 1863." Susan B. Anthony House. Accessed June 10, 2019. https://susanbanthonyhouse.org/blog/wp-content/uploads/2017/07/Susan-B-Anthony-1863.pdf.

AP. "Suffragette's Racial Remark Haunts College." *The New York Times*, May 5, 1996.

Battle, Nishaun T. *Black Girlhood, Punishment, and Resistance: Reimagining Justice for Black Girls in Virginia*. New York: Routledge, 2019.

Bay, Mia. *To Tell the Truth Freely: The Life of Ida B. Wells*. New York: Hill and Wang, 2009.

Bernard, Michelle. "Despite the tremendous risk, African American women marched for suffrage, too." *The Washington Post*, March 3, 2013. Accessed June 1, 2017. https://www.washingtonpost.com/blogs/she-the-people/wp/2013/03/03/despite-the-tremendous-risk-african-american-women-marched-for-suffrage-too/?noredirect=on&utm_term=.866a9fee272f.

Blight, David W. *Frederick Douglass: Prophet of Freedom*. New York: Simon & Schuster, 2018.

Bogan, Ruth, and Bert James Loewenberg. *Black Women in Nineteenth-Century American Life: Their Words, Their Thoughts, Their Feelings*. University Park, Pa.: Pennsylvania State University Press, 1990.

Boissoneault, Lorraine. "The Original Women's March on Washington and the Suffragists Who Paved the Way." *Smithsonian Magazine*, January 23, 2017. Accessed May 12, 2018. https://www.smithsonianmag.com/history/original-womens-march-washington-and-suffragists-who-paved-way-180961869/.

Bordin, Ruth. *Frances Willard: A Biography*. Chapel Hill, N.C.: University of North Carolina Press, 2001.

Boyd, Melba Joyce. *Discarded Legacy: Politics and Poetics in the Life of Frances E. W. Harper, 1825–1911*. Detroit, Mich.: Wayne State University Press, 1994.

Brooks, Maegan Parker, and Davis W. Houck. *The Speeches of Fannie Lou Hamer: To Tell It Like It Is*. Jackson, Miss.: University Press of Mississippi, 2011.

Brower, Kate Andersen. *First Women: The Grace and Power of America's Modern First Ladies*. New York: Harper Collins, 2016.

Brown, Ira V. "Cradle of Feminism: The Philadelphia Female Anti-Slavery Society, 1833–1840." *The Pennsylvania Magazine of History and Biography* 102, no. 2 (April 1978): 143–166.

Brown, Ira V. *Mary Grew: Abolitionist and Feminist (1813–1896)*. Selinsgrove, Pa.: Susquehanna University Press, 1991.

Brown, James, ed. *American Slavery in Its Moral and Political Aspects: Comprehensively Examined: To Which Is Subjoined an Epitome of Ecclesiastical History, Shewing the Mutilated State of Modern Christianity*. n.p.: Palala Press, 2016.

"Call for the First Anniversary of the American Equal Rights Association." Library of Congress. Accessed January 12, 2019. http://www.loc.gov/teachers/classroommaterials/presentationsandactivities/presentations/timeline/civilwar/freedmen/mott.html.

Caraway, Nancie. *Segregated Sisterhood: Racism and the Politics of American Feminism*. Knoxville: University of Tennessee Press, 1991.

Clarke, Kristen, and Ezra Rosenberg. "Trump administration has Voting Rights Act on life support." CNN, August 6, 2018. Accessed February 13, 2019. https://www.cnn.com/2018/08/06/opinions/voting-rights-act-anniversary-long-way-to-go-clarke-rosenberg-opinion/index.html.

Coates, Ta-Nehisi. "The Great Schism." *The Atlantic*, October 18, 2011. Accessed April 3, 2018. https://www.theatlantic.com/national/archive/2011/10/the-great-schism/246640/.

Collier-Thomas, Bettye, and V. P. Franklin, eds. *Sisters in the Struggle: African American Women in the Civil Rights–Black Power Movement*. New York: NYU Press, 2001.

Conkling, Winifred. *Votes for Women!: American Suffragists and the Battle for the Ballot*. Chapel Hill, N.C.: Algonquin Young Readers, 2018.

Cooper, Brittney C. *Beyond Respectability: The Intellectual Thought of Race Women*. Urbana, Ill.: University of Illinois Press, 2017.

Cooper, Valerie C. *Word, Like Fire: Maria Stewart, the Bible, and the Rights of African Americans*. Charlottesville: University of Virginia Press, 2011.

Davis, Angela Y. Women, Race & Class. New York: Vintage, 1983.

Day, Dorothy. *The Long Loneliness: The Autobiography of Dorothy Day*. San Francisco: Harper & Row, 1952.

"The Declaration of Sentiments and Resolutions." National Women's History Museum. Accessed November 10, 2019. https://www.womenshistory.org/resources/primary-source/declaration-sentiments-and-resolution.

DeMuth, Jerry. "Fannie Lou Hamer: Tired of Being Sick and Tired." *The Nation*, June 1, 1964. Accessed November 2, 2018. https://www.thenation.com/article/fannie-lou-hamer-tired-being-sick-and-tired/.

Douglass, Frederick. *The Life and Times of Frederick Douglass*. New York: Penguin Classics, 2014.

Douglass, Frederick. "The Rights of Women." *North Star*, Rochester, July 28, 1848. Accessed March 2, 2019. https://www.loc.gov/exhibits/treasures/images/vc006197.jpg.

Dray, Philip. At the Hands of Person Unknown: The Lynching of Black America. New York: Modern Library 2003.

Du Bois, W. E. B. *The Crisis* 4, no. 2 (July 1912).

Du Bois, W. E. B. *The Crisis* 2, no. 6 (October 1911).

Du Bois, W. E. B. *The Crisis* 11, no. 1 (November 1915).

Dunbar, Erica Armstrong. *A Fragile Freedom: African American Women and Emancipation in the Antebellum City*. New Haven, Conn.: Yale University Press, 2011.

Editorial Board. "The Voting Rights Act at 50." *The New York Times*, August 5, 2015. Accessed October 2, 2019. https://www.nytimes.com/2015/08/05/opinion/the-voting-rights-act-at-50.html.

"Eleanor and Mary Mcleod Bethune." American Experience. Accessed September 12, 2019. http://www.pbs.org/wgbh/americanexperience/features/eleanor-bethune/.

Farnham, Christine Anne, ed. *Women of the American South: A Multicultural Reader*. New York: NYU Press, 1997.

Faulkner, Carol. *Lucretia Mott's Heresy: Abolition and Women's Rights in Nineteenth-Century America*. Philadelphia: University of Pennsylvania Press, 2011.

Fields-White, Monee. "The Root: How Racism Tainted Women's Suffrage." NPR, March 25, 2011. Accessed March 2, 2019. https://www.npr.org/2011/03/25/134849480/the-root-how-racism-tainted-womens-suffrage.

"First National Woman's Rights Convention Ends in Worcester, October 24, 1850." Mass Moments. Accessed April 28, 2019. https://www.massmoments.org/moment-details/first-national-womans-rights-convention-ends-in-worcester.html.

Flexner, Eleanor. *Century of Struggle: The Woman's Rights Movement in the United States*. Cambridge, Mass.: Belknap Press of Harvard University Press, 1959.

Fought, Leigh. *Women in the World of Frederick Douglass*. New York: Oxford University Press, 2017.

Freightman, C. G. "Amelia Boynton Robinson, 104: Fought for voting rights." Atlanta Journal-Constitution, August 26, 2015. https://www.ajc.com/news/breaking-news/amelia-boynton-robinson-104-fought-for-voting-rights/liraycNGE5sf7gc6D2JkYM/.

Garrison, Wendell Phillips, and Francis Jackson Garrison. *William Lloyd Garrison, 1805–1879; the Story of His Life Told by His Children*. Charleston, N.C.: BiblioLife, 2009.

Giddings, Paula J. *Ida: A Sword Among Lions: Ida B. Wells and the Campaign Against Lynching*. New York: Amistad, 2009.

Giddings, Paula. *In Search of Sisterhood: Delta Sigma Theta and the Challenge of the Black Sorority Movement*. New York: William Morrow & Co, 1988.

Giles, Mark S. "Special Focus: Dr. Anna Julia Cooper, 1858–1964: Teacher, Scholar, and Timeless Womanist." *The Journal of Negro Education* 75, no. 4 (Fall 2006): 621–634.

Girard, Jolyon P., Darryl Mace, and Courtney Michelle Smith, eds. *American History through Its Greatest Speeches: A Documentary History of the United States*. Santa Barbara, Cal.: ABC-CLIO, 2017.

Gordon, Ann D, ed. *The Selected Papers of Elizabeth Cady Stanton and Susan B. Anthony: An Awful Hush, 1895 to 1906*. New Brunswick, N.J.: Rutgers University Press, 2013.

Green, Elna C. "The Rest of the Story: Kate Gordon and the Opposition to the Nineteenth Amendment in the South." *The Journal of the Louisiana Historical Association* 33, no. 2 (Spring 1992): 171–189.

Guarino, Ben. "Susan B. Anthony died without the right to vote. Now people are covering her tombstone in 'I voted' stickers." *The Washington Post*, November 8, 2016. Accessed February 28, 2018. https://www.washingtonpost.com/news/ . . . /susan-b-anthony-died-without-the-right-to-\.

Guy-Sheftall, Beverly, ed. *Words of Fire: An Anthology of African-American Feminist Thought*. New York: The New Press, 1995.

GWLI Staff. "Woodrow Wilson and the Women's Suffrage Movement: A Reflection." Global Women's Leadership Initiative. Accessed June 12, 2019. https://www.wilsoncenter.org/article/woodrow-wilson-and-the-womens-suffrage-movement-reflection.

Han, Debra Newman. "African-American Activist Mary Church Terrell and the Brownsville Disturbance." *Trotter Review* 18, no. 1 (2009): 29–44.

Hanks, Lawrence J. *The Struggle for Black Political Empowerment in Three Georgia Counties.* Knoxville, Tenn.: University of Tennessee Press, 1987.

Harley, Sharon, and Rosalyn Terborg-Penn, eds. *The Afro-American Woman: Struggles and Images.* Port Washington, N.Y.: Kennikat Press, 1978.

Harper, Frances Ellen Watkins. "We Are All Bound Up Together—May 1866." Iowa State University, accessed March 13, 2019, https://awpc.cattcenter.iastate.edu/2017/03/21/we-are-all-bound-up-together-may-1866/

Harper, Ida Husted, Susan B. Anthony, and Elizabeth Cady Stanton. *The History of Woman Suffrage.* New York: Fowler & Wells, 1922.

Height, Dorothy I. *Open Wide the Freedom Gates: A Memoir.* New York: PublicAffairs, 2003.

Hendricks, Wanda A. *Fannie Barrier Williams: Crossing the Borders of Region and Race.* Urbana, Ill.: University of Illinois Press, 2014.

Hendricks, Wanda A. *Gender, Race, and Politics in the Midwest: Black Club Women in Illinois.* Bloomington, Ind.: Indiana University Press, 1998.

Hendricks, Wanda A. "'Vote for the Advantage of Ourselves and Our Race': The Election of the First Black Alderman in Chicago." *Illinois Historical Journal* 87, no. 3 (Fall 1994): 171–184.

Henretta, James A., and M. Yazawa, eds. *Documents of America's History; Volume I: To 1877.* New York: Macmillan, 2011.

Higginbotham, Evelyn Brooks. *Righteous Discontent: The Women's Movement in the Black Baptist Church, 1880–1920.* Cambridge, Mass.: Harvard University Press, 1993.

Isenberg, Nancy. *Sex and Citizenship in Antebellum America.* Chapel Hill, N.C.: The University of North Carolina Press, 1998.

Jacobs, Harriet Ann. *The Deeper Wrong: Or, Incidents in the Life of a Slave Girl.* New York: Cambridge University Press, 2011.

Johnson, Kenneth R. "Kate Gordon and the Woman-Suffrage Movement in the South." *The Journal of Southern History* 38, no. 3 (August 1972): 365–392.

Johnson, Lyndon B. "President Johnson's Special Message to the Congress: The American Progress." LBJ Presidential Library, March 15, 1965. http://www.lbjlibrary.org/lyndon-baines-johnson/speeches-films/president-johnsons-special-message-to-the -congress-the-american-promise.

Jones, Beverly W. "Mary Church Terrell and the National Association of Colored Women, 1896 to 1901." *The Journal of Negro History* 67, no. 1 (Spring 1982): 20–33.

Jones, Martha S. *All Bound Up Together: The Woman Question in African American Public Culture, 1830–1900.* Chapel Hill, N.C.: University of North Carolina Press, 2007.

Katagiri, Yasuhiro. *Black Freedom, White Resistance, and Red Menace: Civil Rights and Anticommunism in the Jim Crow South.* Baton Rouge, La.: Louisiana State University Press, 2014.

Kendall, Diana. *The Power of Good Deeds: Privileged Women and the Social Reproduction of the Upper Class.* Lanham, Md.: Rowman & Littlefield Publishers, 2002.

Kendrick, Ruby M. "'They Also Serve': The National Association of Colored Women, Inc." *Negro History Bulletin* 17, no. 8 (May 1954): 171–175. https://www.jstor.org/stable/44214997?read-now=1&seq=5#page_scan_tab_contents.

Kirschke, Amy Helene, and Phillip Luke Sinitiere, eds. *Protest and Propaganda: W. E. B. Du Bois, the "Crisis," and American History.* Columbia, Mo.: University of Missouri, 2014.

Knox, John Barnett. *Address of Hon. John B. Knox: Of Calhoun, on His Installation as President of the Constitutional Convention of Alabama May 22, 1901.* N.p.: Brown Print Company, 1901.

Kucko, John. "Live broadcast: Susan B. Anthony being honored." News 8 WROC Rochester, Facebook, November 8, 2016, https://www.facebook.com/News8WROC/videos/10155359367104386/.

Lemert, Charles, and Esme Bhan, eds. *The Voice of Anna Julia Cooper: Including "A Voice From the South" and Other Important Essays, Papers, and Letters.* Lanham, Md.: Rowman & Littlefield Publishers, 1998.

Lewis, John, and Archie E. Allen. "Black Voter Registration Efforts in the South." *Notre Dame Law Review* 48, no. 1 (1972): 105–132.

Lindhorst, Marie. "Politics in a Box: Sarah Mapps Douglass and the Female Literary Association, 1831–1833." *Pennsylvania History: A Journal of Mid-Atlantic Studies* 65, no. 3 (Summer 1998): 263–278.

Mabee, Carlton, and Susan Mabee Newhouse. *Sojourner Truth: Slave, Prophet, Legend.* New York: NYU Press, 1993.

Magill, Frank Northen. *Great Lives from History: American Women Series*, Volume 5. Pasadena, Calif.: Salem Press, 1995.

Manseau, Peter. "Abolitionist and Reformer Lucretia Mott," National Museum of American History, March 5, 2018. https://americanhistory.si.edu/blog/mott.

Marsh, Charles. *God's Long Summer: Stories of Faith and Civil Rights*. Princeton, N.J.: Princeton University Press, 1997.

Marshall, Schuyler C. "The Free Democratic Convention of 1852." *Pennsylvania History: A Journal of Mid-Atlantic Studies* 22, no. 2 (April 1955): 146–167.

Martin, Earl Devine. *Mary McLeod Bethune: Matriarch of Black America*. Bloomington, Ind.: Xlibris Corporation, 2004.

May, Vivian M. *Anna Julia Cooper, Visionary Black Feminist: A Critical Introduction*. Abingdon, Oxfordshire, England: Routledge, 2007.

McArdle, Terence. "'Night of terror': The suffragists who were beaten and tortured for seeking the vote." *The Washington Post*, November 10, 2017. Accessed August 10, 2018. https://www.washingtonpost.com/news/retropolis/wp/2017/11/10/night-of-terror-the-suffragists-who-were-beaten-and-tortured-for-seeking-the-vote/?utm_term=.9b608232e8c7.

McClymer, John. "How Do Contemporary Newspaper Accounts of the 1850 Worcester Woman's Rights Convention Enhance Our Understanding of the Issues Debated at that Meeting?" in *Women and Social Movements in the United States, 1775–2000*. Binghamton: State University of New York at Binghamton, 2006.

McCluskey, Audrey Thomas. "'We Specialize in the Wholly Impossible': Black Women School Founders and Their Mission," *Signs* 22, no. 2 (Winter 1997), 403–426.

McCluskey, Audrey Thomas, and Elaine M. Smith, eds. *Mary McLeod Bethune: Building a Better World: Essays and Selected Documents*. Bloomington, Ind.: Indiana University Press, 2002.

McDaneld, Jen. "White Suffragist Dis/Entitlement: The *Revolution* and the Rhetoric of Racism." *Legacy* 30, no. 2 (2013): 243–264.

McGuire, Danielle L. *At the Dark End of the Street: Black Women, Rape, and Resistance—a New History of the Civil Rights Movement from Rosa Parks to the Rise of Black Power*. New York: Alfred A. Knopf, 2010.

McHenry, Elizabeth. *Forgotten Readers: Recovering the Lost History of African American Literary Societies*. Durham, N.C.: Duke University Press, 2002.

McMillen, Sally Gregory. *Seneca Falls and the Origins of the Women's Rights Movement*. New York: Oxford University Press, 2008.

McMurry, Linda O. *To Keep the Waters Troubled: The Life of Ida B. Wells*. New York: Oxford University Press, 2000.

"Modern History Sourcebook: Sojourner Truth: 'Ain't I a Woman?' December 1851. Fordham University. Accessed January 12, 2019. https://sourcebooks.fordham.edu/mod/sojtruth-woman.asp.

Morone, James A. *Hellfire Nation: The Politics of Sin in American History*. New Haven: Yale University Press, 2004.

Morrison-Reed, Mark D. *Darkening the Doorways: Black Trailblazers and Missed Opportunities in Unitarian Universalism*. Boston: Skinner House, 2011.

Mott, Lucretia. *Lucretia Mott Speaks: The Essential Speeches and Sermons*. Urbana, Ill.: University of Illinois Press, 2017.

Moye, Todd J. *Let the People Decide: Black Freedom and White Resistance Movements in Sunflower County, Mississippi, 1945–1986*. Chapel Hill, N.C.: University of North Carolina Press, 2004.

Muelder, Owen W. *Theodore Dwight Weld and the American Anti-Slavery Society*. Jefferson, N.C.: McFarland & Company, 2011.

Mukhopadhya, Samhita, and Kate Harding. *Nasty Women: Feminism, Resistance, and Revolution in Trump's America*. New York: Picador, 2017.

"NAACP: A Century in the Fight for Freedom." Library of Congress. Accessed March 5, 2019. https://www.loc.gov/exhibits/naacp/founding-and-early-years.html.

"National Council of Negro Women (NCNW)." The Martin Luther King Jr. Research and Education Institute, Stanford. December 5, 1935. https://kinginstitute.stanford.edu/encyclopedia/national-council-negro-women-ncnw.

"Negro Is Badly Cut." *Illinois State Journal*. 5 Jul 1908.

Newburger, Emma. "Stacey Abrams, after narrow election loss, vows to fight for voter rights," CNBC, March 8, 2019. Accessed August 12, 2019. https://www.cnbc.com/2019/03/08/stacey-abrams-vows-to-fight-for-voter-rights-with-fight-fair-action.html.

Newkirk, Vann R., II. "How *Shelby County v. Holder* Broke America," *The Atlantic*, July 10, 2018. Accessed October 1, 2019. theatlantic.com/politics/archive/2018/07/how-shelby-county-broke-america/564707/.

O'Donnell, Lawrence Jr. *Playing with Fire: The 1968 Election and the Transformation of American Politics*. New York: Penguin Press, 2017.

Painter, Nell Irvin. *Sojourner Truth: A Life, a Symbol*. New York: W. W. Norton & Company, 1996.

Parker, Maegan. "Desiring Citizenship: A Rhetorical Analysis of the Wells-Barnett/Willard Controversy," *Women's Studies in Communication* 31, no. 1 (2008): 56–78.

Perkins, Linda M. "'Bound to Them by a Common Sorrow': African American Women, Higher Education, and Collective Advancement," *The Journal of African American History* 100, no. 4 (Fall 2015), 721–747.

Perreault, Jeanne. "Southern White Women's Autobiographies: Social Equality and Social Change," *The Southern Literary Journal* 41, no. 1 (Fall 2008): 32–51.

Pinder, Sherrow O, ed. *Black Political Thought: From David Walker to the Present.* Cambridge: Cambridge University Press, 2019. Advance copy.

Plummer, Deborah. *Some of My Friends Are . . . :The Daunting Challenges and Untapped Benefits of Cross-Racial Friendships.* Boston: Beacon Press, 2019.

Rhodes, Jane. *Mary Ann Shadd Cary: The Black Press and Protest in the Nineteenth Century.* Bloomington, Ind.: Indiana University Press, 1998.

Richardson, Marilyn, ed. *Maria W. Stewart, America's First Black Woman Political Writer: Essays and Speeches.* Bloomington, Ind.: Indiana University Press, 1987.

Ridley, Jane. "103-year-old activist: I was almost killed fighting for freedom." *New York Post*, December 1, 2014. https://nypost.com/2014/12/01/103-year-old-activist-i-was-almost-killed-fighting-for-freedom/.

Robbins, Hollis, and Henry Louis Gates. *The Portable Nineteenth-Century African American Women Writers.* New York: Penguin Classics, 2017.

Robbins, Jean Marie. "Black Club Women's Purposes for Establishing Kindergartens in the Progressive Era, 1890–1910," PhD diss., Loyola University Chicago, 2011.

Roessner, Lori Amber, and Jodi L. Rightler-McDaniels, eds. *Political Pioneer of the Press: Ida B. Wells-Barnett and Her Transnational Crusade for Social Justice.* Lanham, Md.: Lexington Books, 2018.

Ruffin, Josephine St. Pierre. "Apologists for Lynching." *Woman's Era* 1, no. 3 (June 1894): 14. http://asp6new.alexanderstreet.com.ezproxy.cul.columbia.edu/was2/was2.object.details.aspx?dorpid=1006932720.

Ruiz-Grossman, Sarah, and Sam Levine. "Georgia Candidate Brian Kemp Claims Voter Suppression Is a 'Farce,' Blames Obama," *Huffington Post*, October 23, 2018. Accessed October 12, 2019. https://www.huffpost.com/entry/stacey-abrams-brian-kemp-governor-debate-georgia_n_5bcfd603e4b055bc94860d4d.

Salem, Dorothy C. *To Better Our World: Black Women in Organized Reform, 1890–1920.* Brooklyn, N.Y.: Carlson Pub., 1990.

Schechter, Patricia A. *Ida B. Wells-Barnett and American Reform, 1880–1930.* Chapel Hill, N.C.: The University of North Carolina Press, 2001.

Schumacher, Kris. "Black Women's Struggle For The Suffrage." *Womanspeak* 7, no. 2 (April 1985). https://newspaperarchives.vassar.edu/?a=d&d=Womanspeak19850401-01.2.3.

Scott, Anne Firor. "Most Invisible of All: Black Women's Voluntary Associations." *The Journal of Southern History* 56, no. 1 (February 1990): 3–22.

Shaw, Anna Howard, with Elizabeth Jordan. *The Story of a Pioneer.* New York: Harper & Brothers, 1915.

Specia, Megan. "Overlooked No More: How Mary Ann Shadd Cary Shook Up the Abolitionist Movement." *The New York Times*, June 6, 2018. Accessed April 23, 2019. https://www.nytimes.com/2018/06/06/obituaries/mary-ann-shadd-cary-abolitionist-overlooked.html.

Sprading, Charles T. *Liberty and the Great Libertarians: An Anthology on Liberty, a Hand-Book of Freedom.* San Francisco: Fox & Wilkes, 1995.

St. Pierre, Josephine. "Lady Somerset and Miss Willard Confess of Themselves Apologists for Lynching." *Woman's Era* 2, no. 5 (August 1895).

Stanton, Elizabeth Cady. *Eighty Years and More: Reminiscences, 1815–1897.* New York: Schocken Books, 1971.

Stanton, Elizabeth Cady. *The Greatest Works of Elizabeth Cady Stanton.* n.p.: Madison & Adams Press, 2018.

Stephens, Alexander H. " 'Cornerstone' Speech: Alexander H. Stephens." Teaching American History. Accessed July 6, 2019. https://teachingamericanhistory.org/library/document/cornerstone-speech/.

Stowe, Harriet Beecher. "Sojourner Truth, The Libyan Sibyl: Harriet Beecher Stowe describes her encounter with the legendary African-American activist." *The Atlantic*, April 1863. Accessed May 2, 2019. https://www.theatlantic.com/magazine/archive/1863/04/sojourner-truth-the-libyan-sibyl/308775/.

Strachey, Ray. *Frances Willard, Her Life and Work.* New York: Fleming H. Revell Company, 1913.

Taylor, Elizabeth A. "The Origin of the Woman Suffrage Movement in Georgia." *Georgia Historical Quarterly* 28, no. 2 (June 1944): 63–79.

Taylor, Traki L. "'Womanhood Glorified': Nannie Helen Burroughs and the National Training School for Women and Girls, Inc., 1909–1961." *The Journal of African American History* 87 (Autumn 2002): 392.

Terborg-Penn, Rosalyn. *African American Women in the Struggle for the Vote, 1850–1920*. Bloomington, Ind.: Indiana University Press, 1998.

Terrell, Mary Church. *A Colored Woman in a White World*. Amherst, N.Y.: Humanity Books, 2005.

Tetrault, Lisa. *The Myth of Seneca Falls: Memory and the Women's Suffrage Movement, 1848–1898*. Chapel Hill, N.C.: The University of North Carolina Press, 2014.

Theoharis, Jeanne. *A More Beautiful and Terrible History: The Uses and Misuses of Civil Rights History*. Boston: Beacon Press, 2018.

"This Week in 19th Amendment History: National Woman's Rights Convention." Arlington Public Library. Accessed May 2, 2019. https://library.arlingtonva.us/2019/10/22/this-week-in-19th-amendment-history-national-womans-rights -convention/.

"Today in History—July 19: Seneca Falls Convention." Library of Congress. Accessed February 12, 2019. https://www.loc.gov/item/today-in-history/july-19/.

"Today in History—September 23: Mary Church Terrell." Library of Congress. Accessed August 12, 2019. https://www.loc.gov/item/today-in-history/september-23/.

Truth, Sojourner. *Narrative of Sojourner Truth*. n.p.: Value Classic Reprints, 2017.

Tuuri, Rebecca. *Strategic Sisterhood: The National Council of Negro Women in the Black Freedom Struggle*. Chapel Hill, N.C.: The University of North Carolina Press, 2018.

Tyrrell, Ian. *Woman's World/Woman's Empire: The Woman's Christian Temperance Union in International Perspective, 1880–1930*. Chapel Hill, N.C.: The University of North Carolina Press, 1991.

United States Commission on Civil Rights. "An Assessment of Minority Voting Rights Access in the United States." September 12, 2018. https://www.usccr.gov/press/2018/09-12-18-PR.pdf.

Vetter, Lisa Pace. *The Political Thought of America's Founding Feminists*. New York: NYU Press, 2017.

Wagner, Sally Roesch, ed. *The Women's Suffrage Movement*. New York: Penguin Classics, 2019.

Walton, Mary. "The Day the Deltas Marched into History." *The Washington Post*, March 1, 2013. Accessed August 2, 2018. https://www.washingtonpost.com/opinions/the-day-the-deltas-marched-into-history/2013/03/01/eabbf130-811d-11e2-b99e -6baf4ebe42df_story.html?utm_term=.5be8ca83e8c.

Watson, Martha Solomon. "Mary Church Terrell vs. Thomas Nelson Page: Gender, Race, and Class in Anti-Lynching Rhetoric." *Rhetoric and Public Affairs* 12, no. 1 (Spring 2009): 65–89.

Webber, Christopher L. *American to the Backbone: The Life of James W. C. Pennington, the Fugitive Slave Who Became One of the First Black Abolitionists*. New York: Pegasus Books, 2011.

Weiss, Penny A., and Megan Brueske, eds. *Feminist Manifestos: A Global Documentary Reader*. New York: NYU Press, 2018.

Wells, Ida B. *Crusade for Justice: The Autobiography of Ida B. Wells*. Chicago: University of Chicago Press, 1991.

Wells, Ida B. "Lynching Our National Crime—June 1, 1909." Iowa State University: Archives of Women's Political Communication. Accessed February 19, 2019. https://awpc.cattcenter.iastate.edu/2017/03/09/mob-murder-in-a-christian-nation-june-1-1909/.

Wells-Barnett, Ida B. *Southern Horrors: Lynch Law in All Its Phases*. n.p.: CreateSpace Independent Publishing Platform, 2017.

Wesley, Charles H. *The History of the National Association of Colored Women's Clubs: A Legacy of Service*. Washington, D.C.: National Association of Colored Women's Clubs, 1984.

Wheeler, Marjorie Spruill. *New Women of the New South: The Leaders of the Woman Suffrage Movement in the Southern States*. New York: Oxford University Press, 1993.

White, Deborah Gray. *Too Heavy a Load: Black Women in Defense of Themselves, 1894–1994*. New York: W. W. Norton & Company, 1999.

Willard, Frances Elizabeth. "Fifteenth Presidential Address (1894)." In *Let Something Good Be Said: Speeches and Writing of Frances E. Willard*. Ed. Carolyn De Swarte Gifford and Amy R. Slagell. Champaign: University of Illinois Press, 2007.

Yaeger, Lynn. "The African-American Suffragists History Forgot." *Vogue*, October 21, 2015. Accessed April 1, 2019. https://www.vogue.com/article/african-american-suffragists-women-voting-rights.

Yates, Josephine Silone. "Kindergartens and mothers' clubs as related to the work of the National Association of Colored Women." *The Colored American Magazine* 9, no. 6 (June 1905): 304–311.

Yates, Josephine Silone. "Report of the National Association of Colored Women's Clubs to the National Council of Women at Washington." *The Colored American Magazine* 9, no. 6 (June 1905): 258–262.

Yee, Shirley J. *Black Women Abolitionists: A Study in Activism, 1828–1860*. Knoxville, Tenn.: University of Tennessee Press, 1992.

Yellin, Jean Fagan. "Dubois' 'Crisis' and Woman's Suffrage." *The Massachusetts Review* 14, no. 2 (Spring 1973): 365–375.

Yellin, Jean Fagan, and John C. Van Horne, eds. *The Abolitionist Sisterhood: Women's Political Culture in Antebellum America.* Ithaca, N.Y.: Cornell University Press, 1994.

Zackodnik, Teresa C. " 'I Don't Know How You Will Feel When I Get Through': Racial Difference, Woman's Rights, and Sojourner Truth." *Feminist Studies* 30, no. 1 (Spring 2004): 47–73.

Zackodnik, Teresa C. *"We Must Be Up and Doing": A Reader in Early African American Feminisms.* Peterborough, Ont.: Broadview Press, 2010.

Zahniser, J. D., and Amelia R. Fry. *Alice Paul: Claiming Power.* New York: Oxford University Press, 2019.

Sources

Preface

"This is so powerful . . . there's never been a line": Deborah Hughes, interview by John Kucko, "Live broadcast: Susan B. Anthony being honored," News 8 WROC Rochester, Facebook, November 8, 2016, https://www.facebook.com/News8WROC/videos/10155359367104386/.

Chapter 1: Abolitionist Women Embrace the Fight

"Enslave the liberty of . . .": Charles T. Sprading, ed., "VIII: William Lloyd Garrison," in *Liberty and the Great Libertarians: An Anthology on Liberty, a Hand-Book of Freedom*. (San Francisco: Fox & Wilkes, 1995), 154.

"Whether we turn to the declarations of the past . . . false to the future": James A. Henretta and Melvin Yazawa, eds. "Frederick Douglass, What to the Slave is the Fourth of July? (1852)," in *Documents for America's History, Volume I: To 1877*, ed. (New York: Macmillan, 2011), 275.

"It is true, the wail of the captive . . .": Elizabeth McHenry, *Forgotten Readers: Recovering the Lost History of African American Literary Societies* (Durham, N.C.: Duke University Press, 2002), 59.

"recite and read": Marie Lindhorst, "Politics in a Box: Sarah Mapps Douglass and the Female Literary Association, 1831–1833," *Pennsylvania History: A Journal of Mid-Atlantic Studies* 65, no. 3 (Summer 1998): 270.

"endeavors to enlighten the understanding . . .": Lindhorst, *Pennsylvania History* 65, no. 3: 269.

"civil and religious privileges": Owen W. Muelder, *Theodore Dwight Weld and the American Anti-Slavery Society* (Jefferson, N.C.: McFarland & Company, 2011), 9.

"heinous crime in the sight of God": James Brown, ed., "Review of Mr. Clay's Speech on Slavery," in *American Slavery in Its Moral and Political Aspects: Comprehensively Examined: To Which Is Subjoined an Epitome of Ecclesiastical History, Shewing the Mutilated State of Modern Christianity* (n.p.: Palala Press, 2016), 9.

"We are all bound up together . . .": Martha S. Jones, *All Bound Up Together: The Woman Question in African American Public Culture, 1830–1900* (Chapel Hill, N. C.: The University of North Carolina Press, 2007), iv.

"I claim for the negro protection in every right . . . political life and ranks": Ruth Bogin and Bert James Loewenberg, eds., Frances Ellen Watkins Harper, "Let Us Make a Mighty Effort and Arise," in *Black Women in Nineteenth-Century American Life: Their Words, Their Thoughts, Their Feelings.* (University Park, Pa.: Pennsylvania State University Press, 1990), 248.

"elevate the people of color from their present degraded situation . . .": Elizabeth Cady Stanton, *The Greatest Works of Elizabeth Cady Stanton* (n.p.: Madison & Adams Press, 2018).

"contrary to the laws of God": Erica Armstrong Dunbar, *A Fragile Freedom: African American Women and Emancipation in the Antebellum City* (New Haven, Conn.: Yale University Press, 2011), 85.

"[We] lived together in a comfortable home . . .": Harriet Ann Jacobs, *The Deeper Wrong: Or, Incidents in the Life of a Slave Girl* (New York: Cambridge University Press, 2011), 5.

"foul words": Jacobs, *The Deeper Wrong*, 44.

"deliberate calculation . . . control over you": Jacobs, *The Deeper Wrong*, 83.

"Whatever slavery might do to me . . . little ones were saved": Jacobs, *The Deeper Wrong*, 166.

"correct information": Nancy Isenberg, *Sex and Citizenship in Antebellum America* (Chapel Hill, N.C.: The University of North Carolina Press, 1998), 59.

"this foul stain": Ira V. Brown, "Cradle of Feminism: The Philadelphia Female Anti-Slavery Society, 1833–1840," *The Pennsylvania Magazine of History and Biography* 102, no. 2 (April 1978): 146.

"if she would do well and be faithful": Sojourner Truth, *Narrative of Sojourner Truth* (n.p.: Value Classic Reprints, 2017), 18.

"I did not run off . . .": Carleton Mabee and Susan Mabee Newhouse, *Sojourner Truth: Slave, Prophet, Legend* (New York: NYU Press, 1993), 13.

"The Lord gave me [the name] Sojourner . . .": Teresa C. Zackodnik, ed., Sojourner Truth, "Sojourner Truth (1863)," in *We Must Be Up and Doing": A Reader in Early African American Feminisms.* (Peterborough, Ont.: Broadview Press, 2010), 292.

"All of the nations of the earth are crying out . . .": Marilyn Richardson, ed., Maria W. Stewart, "Introduction," in *Maria W. Stewart, America's First Black Woman Political Writer: Essays and Speeches.* (Bloomington, Ind.: Indiana University Press, 1987), 9.

"O, ye daughters of Africa! . . .": Richardson, *Maria W. Stewart*, 30.

"expedient and desirable": Ira V. Brown, *Mary Grew: Abolitionist and Feminist (1813–1896)* (Selinsgrove, Pa.: Susquehanna University Press, 1991), 16.

"the duty of every human being to labor to preserve . . .": Penny A. Weiss and Megan Brueske, eds., "Resolutions," *Feminist Manifestos: A Global Documentary Reader* (New York: NYU Press, 2018), 58.

"the duty of woman, and the province of woman . . .": Harriet Hyman Alonso, *Peace as Women's Issue: A History of the U.S. Movement for World Peace and Women's Rights* (Syracuse, N.Y.: Syracuse University Press, 1993), 31.

Chapter 2: "Ain't I a Woman?" The Cult of True Womanhood

"To put a woman on the committee with men . . .": Christopher L. Webber, *American to the Backbone: The Life of James W. C. Pennington, the Fugitive Slave Who Became One of the First Black Abolitionists* (New York: Pegasus Books, 2011).

"We should not be surprised if she should so far forget the true dignity . . .": Peter Manseau, "Abolitionist and Reformer Lucretia Mott," *National Museum of American History*, March 5, 2018, https://americanhistory.si.edu/blog/mott.

"never lose sight of their familial responsibilities . . .": Shirley J. Yee, *Black Women Abolitionists: A Study in Activism, 1828–1860* (Knoxville, Tenn.: University of Tennessee Press, 1992), 40.

"daughters are destined to be wives and mothers . . .": Yee, *Black Women Abolitionists*, 50.

"densely crowded": Schuyler C. Marshall, "The Free Democratic Convention of 1852," *Pennsylvania History: A Journal of Mid-Atlantic Studies* 22, no. 2 (April 1955): 150.

"form a society to advocate for the rights of women": Elizabeth Cady Stanton, *Eighty Years and More Reminiscences, 1815–1897* (New York: Schocken Books, 1971), 83.

"from our best families . . .": Dunbar, *A Fragile Freedom*, 61.

"We are assembled to protest against a form of government . . .": "Today in History—July 19: Seneca Falls Convention," Library of Congress, accessed February 12, 2019, https://www.loc.gov/item/today-in-history/july-19/.

"all men and women . . .": The Declaration of Sentiments and Resolutions, National Women's History Museum, accessed November 10, 2019, https://www.womenshistory.org/resources/primary-source/declaration-sentiments-and-resolution.

"That it is the duty of women . . .": "The Declaration of Sentiments and Resolutions."

"I have never yet been able to find one consideration . . .": Frederick Douglass, *The Life and Times of Frederick Douglass* (New York: Penguin Classics, 2014), 346.

"In respect to political rights . . .": Frederick Douglass, "The Rights of Women," *North Star*, July 28, 1848, https://www.loc.gov/exhibits/treasures/images/vc006197.jpg.

"We should do more and talk less . . . considering our resolve": Megan Specia, "Overlooked No More: How Mary Ann Shadd Cary Shook Up the Abolitionist Movement," *The New York Times*, June 6, 2018, https://www.nytimes.com/2018/06/06/obituaries/mary-ann-shadd-cary-abolitionist-overlooked.html.

"I conceive that the first thing to be done . . .": Wendell Phillips Garrison and Francis Jackson Garrison, *William Lloyd Garrison, 1805–1879; the Story of His Life Told by His Children* (Charleston, N.C.: BiblioLife, 2009), 310.

"to secure for [woman] political, legal, and social equality with man . . .": National American Woman Suffrage Association, "The proceedings of the Woman's Rights Convention at Worcester, October 23rd & 24th, 1850," Library of Congress, accessed March 12, 2019, https://www.loc.gov/item/93838286/.

"trampled women of the plantation": "First National Woman's Rights Convention Ends in Worcester, October 24, 1850," Mass Moments, accessed April 28, 2019, https://www.massmoments.org/moment-details/first-national-womans-rights-convention-ends-in-worcester.html.

"bear down a whole audience with a few simple words": Harriet Beecher Stowe, "Sojourner Truth, The Libyan Sibyl: Harriet Beecher Stowe describes her encounter with the legendary African-American activist," *The Atlantic*, April 1863, https://www.theatlantic.com/magazine/archive/1863/04/sojourner-truth-the-libyan-sibyl/308775/.

"a woman was just as well qualified . . .": John McClymer, "*How Do Contemporary Newspaper Accounts of the 1850 Worcester Woman's Rights Convention Enhance Our Understanding of the Issues Debated at that Meeting?*" Women and Social Movements in the United States, 1775–2000 (Binghamton: State University of New York at Binghamton, 2006).

"abolish the bible . . . of sexes and colors": "This Week in 19th Amendment History: National Woman's Rights Convention," Arlington Public Library, accessed May 2, 2019, https://library.arlingtonva.us/2019/10/22/this-week-in-19th-amendment-history-national-womans-rights-convention/.

"That man over there . . . the men better let them": "Modern History Sourcebook: Sojourner Truth: 'Ain't I a Woman?' December 1851, Fordham University, accessed January 12, 2019 https://sourcebooks.fordham.edu/mod/sojtruth-woman.asp

Chapter 3: The Negro Hour Is Upon Us

"proper status of the negro in our form of civilization": Alexander H. Stephens, "'Cornerstone' Speech: Alexander H. Stephens," Teaching American History, accessed July 6, 2019, https://teachingamericanhistory.org/library/document/cornerstone-speech/.

"There is great fear expressed on all sides . . .": Susan B. Anthony, "Susan B. Anthony's Return to the 'Old Union' speech, 1863," Susan B. Anthony House, accessed June 10, 2019, https://susanbanthonyhouse.org/blog/wp-content/uploads/2017/07/Susan-B-Anthony-1863.pdf.

"we must up take but one question at a time . . .": Lisa Pace Vetter, The Political Thought of America's Founding Feminists (New York: NYU Press, 2017), 185.

"I do not believe . . .": Frances Ellen Watkins Harper, "We Are All Bound Up Together—May 1866," Iowa State University, accessed March 13, 2019, https://awpc.cattcenter.iastate.edu/2017/03/21/we-are-all-bound-up-together-may-1866/.

"secure Equal Rights to all American citizens . . .": "Call for the First Anniversary of the American Equal Rights Association," Library of Congress, accessed January 12, 2019, http://www.loc.gov/teachers/classroommaterials/presentationsandactivities/presentations/timeline/civilwar/freedmen/mott.html.

"I feel that I have the right . . .": Lynn Yaeger, "The African-American Suffragists History Forgot," Vogue, October 21, 2015, https://www.vogue.com/article/african-american-suffragists-women-voting-rights.

"The old anti-slavery school say . . .": Amy Helene Kirschke and Phillip Luke Sinitiere, eds., Protest and Propaganda: W. E. B. Du Bois, the 'Crisis', and American History (Columbia, Mo.: University of Missouri, 2019), 139.

"I will cut off my right arm . . .": Samhita Mukhopadhya and Kate Harding, Nasty Women: Feminism, Resistance, and Revolution in Trump's America (New York: Picador, 2017), 18.

"The enfranchisement of women . . .": Jeanne Perreault, "Southern White Women's Autobiographies: Social Equality and Social Change," The Southern Literary Journal 41, no. 1 (Fall 2008): 38.

"Your 4,000,000 Southern white women . . .": Angela Y. Davis, Women, Race & Class (New York: Vintage, 1983), 114.

"hunted down through the cities of New York and New Orleans . . . equal to our own": Leigh Fought, Women in the World of Frederick Douglass (New York: Oxford University Press, 2017), 198.

"You have put the ballot in the hands . . .": Anna Howard Shaw, with Elizabeth Jordan, The Story of a Pioneer (New York: Harper & Brothers, 1915), 312.

"airy nothings and selfishness": Nell Irvin Painter, Sojourner Truth: A Life, a Symbol (New York: W.W. Norton & Company, 1996), 225.

"one and universal . . . the chain is broken": Charles Lemert and Esme Bhan, eds., Anna Julia Cooper, "Intellectual Progress of Colored Women," in The Voice of Anna Julia Cooper: Including "A Voice From the South" and Other Important Essays, Papers, and Letters (Lanham, Md.: Rowman & Littlefield Publishers, 1998), 205.

"intellectual development, with the self-reliance and capacity . . .": Lemert, The Voice of Anna Julia Cooper, 82.

"I constantly felt (as I suppose many an ambitious girl has felt) . . .": Lemert, The Voice of Anna Julia Cooper, 86.

"remov[ed] property requirements for voting . . . free public school systems": Lawrence J. Hanks, The Struggle for Black Political Empowerment in Three Georgia Counties (Knoxville, Tenn.: University of Tennessee Press, 1987), 14.

"ignore the priorities of Black women . . .": Rosalyn Terborg-Penn, African American Women in the Struggle for the Vote, 1850–1920 (Bloomington, Ind.: Indiana University Press, 1998), 56.

"negro domination": Marjorie Spruill Wheeler, New Women of the New South: The Leaders of the Woman Suffrage Movement in the Southern States (New York: Oxford University Press, 1993), 129.

"only honorable solution of white supremacy in the South": Ann D. Gordon, ed., .Kate Gordon, "18 March 1903," in The Selected Papers of Elizabeth Cady Stanton and Susan B. Anthony: An Awful Hush, 1895 to 1906 (New Brunswick, N.J.: Rutgers University Press, 2013), 470.

"All taxpaying women shall have . . .": Elizabeth Cady Stanton, The History of Woman Suffrage, Volume 4 (1902), 681.

Chapter 4: The Rise of Black Women's Suffrage Clubs

"Our job was to go to school and learn all we could": Lori Amber Roessner and Jodi L. Rightler-McDaniels, eds., Ida B. Wells-Barnett, "Training the Pen: Ida B. Wells' Journalistic Efforts to Combat Emerging Jim Crow Laws in Transportation," in Political Pioneer of the Press: Ida B. Wells-Barnett and Her Transnational Crusade for Social Justice (Lanham, Md.: Lexington Books, 2018), 6.

"I had braced my feet . . . try it again by himself": Roessener and Rightler-McDaniels, 4.

"Hundreds left on foot . . . to punish lynchers": Jolyon P. Girard, Darryl Mace, and Courtney Michelle Smith, eds., Ida B. Wells-Barnett, "Lynch Law in All Its Phrases," in *American History through Its Greatest Speeches: A Documentary History of the United States* (Santa Barbara, Cal.: ABC-CLIO, 2017), 269.

"I have no power to describe . . .": Girard, Mace, and Smith, 270.

"sober and pure world": Ian Tyrrell, *Woman's World/Woman's Empire: The Woman's Christian Temperance Union in International Perspective, 1880–1930* (Chapel Hill, N.C.: The University of North Carolina Press, 1991), 7.

"'Better whiskey and more of it' is the rallying cry . . . in a thousand localities": James A. Morone, *Hellfire Nation: The Politics of Sin in American History* (New Haven: Yale University Press, 2004), 246.

"I pity the southerners . . .": Morone, *Hellfire Nation,* 246.

"alien illiterates . . . the price of his own mule": Morone, *Hellfire Nation*, 246.

"put an imputation upon half . . .": Morone, *Hellfire Nation*, 246.

"Our duty to the colored people have [sic] never impressed me . . .": Ruth Bordin, *Frances Willard: A Biography* (Chapel Hill, N.C.: University of North Carolina Press, 2001), 216.

"true lover of the Southern People": Philip Dray, *At the Hands of Person Unknown: The Lynching of Black America* (New York: Modern Library 2003), 106.

"delightful, helpful": Mary Church Terrell, *A Colored Woman in a White World* (Amherst, N.Y.: Humanity Books, 2005), 185.

"until you hold a convention in the South . . . women do not want the ballot": Elizabeth A. Taylor, "The Origin of the Woman Suffrage Movement in Georgia," *Georgia Historical Quarterly* 28, no. 2 (June 1944): 69.

"go away with NAWSA membership tickets in their pockets": Taylor, *Georgia Historical Quarterly*: 69.

"Men alone, white and Black, have the privilege . . .": Ida Husted Harper, Susan B. Anthony, and Elizabeth Cady Stanton, eds., Mary Latimer McLendon, "National-American Convention of 1895," in *The History of Woman Suffrage.* (New York: Fowler & Wells, 1922), 242.

"make the Solid South a friend to woman suffrage": Taylor, *Georgia Historical Quarterly*: 69.

"I did not want to subject him to humiliation . . .": Ida B. Wells, *Crusade for Justice: The Autobiography of Ida B. Wells* (Chicago: University of Chicago Press, 1991), 230.

"illiterate citizens": Sally Roesch Wagner, ed., Elizabeth Cady Stanton, "Woman's Imperative Duty," in *The Women's Suffrage Movement* (New York: Penguin Classics, 2019), 407.

"While we were reciting our history lesson one day . . . humiliated and disgraced": Anne Firor Scott, "Most Invisible of All: Black Women's Voluntary Associations," *The Journal of Southern History* 56, no. 1 (February 1990): 6.

"show those white girls and boys . . .": Scott, *The Journal of Southern History*: 6.

"organizing themselves for self-help": Scott, *The Journal of Southern History*: 6.

"obliged to be politic, and for the Welfare of the WCTU . . . tremendous organization": Josephine St. Pierre, "Lady Somerset and Miss Willard Confess of Themselves Apologists for Lynching," *Woman's Era* 2, no. 5 (August 1895): 17.

"[They are] up to their ears in guilt . . .": Josephine St. Pierre Ruffin, "Apologists for Lynching," *Woman's Era* 1, no. 3 (June 1894): 14.

"It is inconceivable that the WTCU . . .": Frances Elizabeth Willard, "Fifteenth Presidential Address (1894)," in *Let Something Good Be Said: Speeches and Writing of Frances E. Willard*, ed. Carolyn De Swarte Gifford and Amy R. Slagell (Champaign: University of Illinois Press, 2007), 204.

"no sense of virtue . . . natural thieves and liars": Beverly W. Jones, "Mary Church Terrell and the National Association of Colored Women, 1896 to 1901," *The Journal of Negro History* 67, no. 1 (Spring 1982): 22–23.

"stirred the intelligent colored woman of America . . . good as other American women": Wanda A. Hendricks, *Gender, Race, and Politics in the Midwest: Black Club Women in Illinois* (Bloomington, Ind.: Indiana University Press, 1998), 19.

"Five years ago we had no colored women's club . . .": Hollis Robbins and Henry Louis Gates, eds., Josephine St. Pierre Ruffin, "Address to the First National Conference of Colored Women (1895)," *The Portable Nineteenth-Century African American Women Writers* (New York: Penguin Classics, 2017), 169.

"feel the cheer and inspiration . . .": Robbins and Gates, *The Portable Nineteenth-Century*, 169.

"the things that are of special interest . . .": Nishaun T. Battle, *Black Girlhood, Punishment, and Resistance: Reimagining Justice for Black Girls in Virginia* (New York: Routledge, 2019).

"standing for purity and mental worth": Robbins and Gates, *The Portable Nineteenth-Century*, 171.

"equip ourselves with knowledge . . .": Hendricks, *Gender, Race, and Politics*, 19.

"awaken the women of the race . . . effort in home-making": Linda M. Perkins, "'Bound to Them by a Common Sorrow': African American Women, Higher Education, and Collective Advancement," *The Journal of African American History* 100, no. 4 (Fall 2015): 727.

"Not only are colored women with ambition . . . meeting them at every turn": "Today in History—September 23: Mary Church Terrell," Library of Congress, accessed August 12, 2019, https://www.loc.gov/item/today-in-history/september-23/.

"Colored women who are working . . .": Robbins and Gates, *The Portable Nineteenth Century*, 439.

Chapter 5: Voting Is Only for Educated Women

"to secure harmony of action and cooperation . . .": Jones, *The Journal of Negro History*: 26.

"The daily clinics have been a great blessing . . .": Sherrow O. Pinder, ed., Mary Church Terrell, "The Progress of Colored Women," in *Black Political Thought: From David Walker to the Present* (Cambridge: Cambridge University Press, 2019), 224.

Traki L. Taylor, "'Womanhood Glorified': Nannie Helen Burroughs and the National Training School for Women and Girls, Inc., 1909-1961," *The Journal of African American History* 87 (Autumn 2002), 392.

"And so, lifting as we climb, onward . . . asking an equal chance": Pinder, *Black Political Thought*, 226.

"The question of white supremacy . . .": Elna C. Green, "The Rest of the Story: Kate Gordon and the Opposition to the Nineteenth Amendment in the South," *Louisiana History: The Journal of the Louisiana Historical Association* 33, no. 2 (Spring 1992): 174.

"black eye to the woman suffrage . . .": Wheeler, *New Women of the New South*, 123.

"the city dump and the trash piles behind hotels": Earl Devine Martin, *Mary McLeod Bethune: Matriarch of Black America* (Bloomington, Ind.: Xlibris Corporation, 2004), 37.

"light colored negro with a slight mustache": James L. Crouthamel, "The Springfield Race Riot of 1908," *The Journal of Negro History* no. 3 (July 1960): 167.

"I believe that the greatest hope . . .": Audrey Thomas McCluskey, "'We Specialize in the Wholly Impossible': Black Women School Founders and Their Mission," *Signs* 22, no. 2 (Winter 1997): 411.

"our national crime": R.J. Vogt, "Pioneering Advocacy Journalism: What Today's Journalists Can Learn from Ida B. Wells-Barnett's Methodology," in Roessner and Rightler-McDaniels, *Political Pioneer of the Press*, 142.

"The only certain remedy [to lynching] . . . state in which he belongs": Ida B. Wells, "Lynching Our National Crime—June 1, 1909," Iowa State University: Archives of Women's Political Communication, accessed February 19, 2019, https://awpc.cattcenter.iastate.edu/2017/03/09/mob-murder-in-a-christian-nation-june-1-1909/.

"promote equality of rights . . .": "NAACP: A Century in the Fight for Freedom." Library of Congress, accessed March 5, 2019, https://www.loc.gov/exhibits/naacp/founding-and-early-years.html.

"votes for women means votes for Black women": Jean Fagan Yellin, "Dubois' 'Crisis' and Woman's Suffrage," *The Massachusetts Review* 14, no. 2 (Spring 1973): 368.

"the conduct of educational systems . . .": Yellin, *The Massachusetts Review*, 368

"I do not feel that we should go into a Southern State . . .": Hendricks, *Gender, Race, and Politics*, 76.

"I am in favor of colored people voting . . .": W. E. B. Du Bois, *The Crisis* 4, no. 2 (July 1912): 77.

"The nemesis of every forward movement . . .": W. E. B. Du Bois, *The Crisis* 2, no. 6 (October 1911): 243.

"barefaced falsehood. . . not according to their color": Du Bois, *The Crisis* 2, no. 6: 244.

"There is not . . . president of the National Association": Du Bois, *The Crisis* 4, no. 2: 76.

"wholly inadequate": W. E. B. Du Bois, *The Crisis* 11, no. 1 (November 1915): 42.

"Black cause with the woman suffrage cause": Amy Helene Kirschke and Phillip Luke Sinitiere, eds., W. E. B. Du Bois, "W. E. B. Du Bois and 'The Crisis' of Woman Suffrage," in *Protest and Propaganda: W. E. B. Du Bois, the "Crisis," and American History* (Columbia, Mo.: University of Missouri, 2019), 146.

"trying to lift themselves . . .": Kris Schumacher, "Black Women's Struggle For The Suffrage," *Womanspeak* 7, no. 2 (April 1985): 10, https://newspaperarchives.vassar.edu/?a=d&d=Womanspeak19850401-01.2.3.

"Let every Black man and woman fight": Kirschke and Sinitiere, *Protest and Propaganda*, 146.

Chapter 6: Taking It to the Streets

"we [women] could use our vote . . .": Roessner and Rightler, *Political Pioneer of the Press*, 67.

"for the advantage of ourselves and our race": Wanda A. Hendricks, "'Vote for the Advantage of Ourselves and Our Race': The Election of the First Black Alderman in Chicago," *Illinois Historical Journal* 87, no. 3 (Fall 1994): 173.

"sweet and delightful": Mark D. Morrison-Reed, *Darkening the Doorways: Black Trailblazers and Missed Opportunities in Unitarian Universalism* (Boston: Skinner House, 2011), 30.

"there could not have been a relationship . . .": Fannie Barrier Williams, "A Northern Negro's Autobiography," *The Independent*, Volume 57, (n.p., July to December 1904), 91.

"the hearts of Afro-American women . . . elevation of all the people": Robbins and Gates, Fannie Barrier Williams, "The Intellectual Progress of the Colored Woman of the United States since the Emancipation Proclamation (1893)," in *The Portable Nineteenth-Century African American Women Writers*, 398.

"ought to be at home taking care of the babies . . . and 'wear their trousers'": Terborg-Penn, *African American Women in the Struggle for the Vote*, 99.

"the women's vote was a revelation . . .": Hendricks, "'Vote for the Advantage of Ourselves and Our Race,'" 173.

Chapter 7: The Back of the Movement: The Women's Suffrage March

"unalterably opposed to militancy . . .": Frank Northen Magill, *Great Lives from History: American Women Series*, Volume 5 (Pasadena, Calif.: Salem Press, 1995), 1639.

"of fine dignity . . .": Kimberly A. Hamlin, "The First Time Women Marched on Washington," *Origins: Current Events in Historical Events*, accessed March 8, 2019, https://origins.osu.edu/connecting-history /first-time-women-marched-washington.

"refrain from publishing anything . . . disastrous effect": Ama Ansah, "Votes for Women Means Votes for Black Women," National Women's History Museum, accessed March 11, 2019, https://www.womenshistory.org/articles /votes-women-means-votes-black-women.

"say nothing whatever about the [negro] question . . .": J. D. Zahniser and Amelia R. Fry, *Alice Paul: Claiming Power* (New York: Oxford University Press, 2019), 138.

"service for all mankind": Mission Statement, Alpha Kappa Alpha, https://aka1908.com/about/mission.

"so strongly [urging] Colored women . . .": Ansah, "Votes for Women means Votes for Black Women."

"If the Illinois women do not take a stand . . .": Roessner and Rightler, *Political Pioneer of the Press*, 68.

"unless I can march under the Illinois banner": Roessner and Rightler, *Political Pioneer of the Press*, 68.

"Men, many of them drunk . . .": Mary Walton, "The day the Deltas Marched into History," *The Washington Post*, March 1, 2013, https://www.washingtonpost.com/opinions/the-day-the-deltas-marched-into-history/2013/03/01/eabbf130-811d-11e2 -b99e-6baf4ebe42df_story.html.

"our young giant Oscar DePriest . . .": Linda O. McMurry, *To Keep the Waters Troubled: The Life of Ida B. Wells* (New York: Oxford University Press, 2000), 311.

"to leave no stone unturned": Roessner and Rightler, *Political Pioneer of the Press*, 72.

"only group in this country . . .": Terborg-Penn, *African American Women in the Struggle for the Vote*, 158.

"first, because we are women . . .": Terborg-Penn, *African American Women in the Struggle for the Vote*, 97.

"strengthened, not weakened, by women's suffrage": AP, "Suffragette's Racial Remark Haunts College," *The New York Times*, May 5, 1996.

"We have made partners . . . privilege and right": GWLI Staff, "Woodrow Wilson and the Women's Suffrage Movement: A Reflection," Global Women's Leadership Initiative, accessed June 12, 2019, https://www.wilsoncenter.org/article /woodrow-wilson-and-the-womens-suffrage-movement-reflection.

"When the forcible feeding . . .": "Alice Paul Talks," *Philadelphia Tribune*, (Philadelphia, 1910), https://www.loc.gov/resource/rbcmil.scrp6014202/?st=text.

"In the morning we were taken . . .": Dorothy Day, *The Long Loneliness: The Autobiography of Dorothy Day* (San Francisco: Harper & Row, 1952), 69.

Chapter 8: Voting Out Jim Crow

"to establish white supremacy in this state . . .": John Barnett Knox, *Address of Hon. John B. Knox: Of Calhoun, on His Installation as President of the Constitutional Convention of Alabama, May 22, 1901* (n.p.: Brown Print. Company, 1901), 4.

"improve their own condition and that of their race": Ruby M. Kendrick, "'They Also Serve': The National Association of Colored Women, Inc.," *Negro History Bulletin* 17, no. 8 (May 1954): 171.

"conditions for family living": Diana Kendall, *The Power of Good Deeds: Privileged Women and the Social Reproduction of the Upper Class* (Lanham, Md.: Rowman & Littlefield Publishers, 2002), 148.

"especially interested in the problems of women of color . . .": Kendrick, *Negro History Bulletin*, 172.

"her closest friend in her age group": Deborah Plummer, *Some of My Friends Are. . . . : The Daunting Challenges and Untapped Benefits of Cross-Racial Friendships* (Boston: Beacon Press, 2019), 14.

"learn the simples of farming . . .": "Eleanor and Mary Mcleod Bethune," American Experience, accessed September 12, 2019, http://www.pbs.org/wgbh/americanexperience/features/eleanor-bethune/.

"competent and courageous leadership among negro women": Christie Anne Farnham, ed., Mary McLeod Bethune, "Black Women's Culture of Resistance and the Right to Vote," in Women of the American South: A Multicultural Reader, ed. (New York: NYU Press, 1997), 215.

"We have had a chance to look down . . . to roll for Negroes": McCluskey and Smith, Mary McLeod Bethune, "Minutes of the Federal Council on Negro Affairs (1936)," in Mary McLeod Bethune: Building a Better World, 227.

"She drew me into her dazzling orbit . . . 'We must pry them fully open'": Dorothy I. Height, Open Wide the Freedom Gates: A Memoir (New York: PublicAffairs, 2003), 83.

"I feel a sense of peace . . . have moved mountains": McCluskey and Smith, eds. Mary McLeod Bethune, "Stepping Aside . . . at Seventy-Four (1949)," in Mary McLeod Bethune, 193.

"long admired this organization. . .": "National Council of Negro Women (NCNW)," The Martin Luther King Jr. Research and Education Institute, Stanford, December 5, 1935, https://kinginstitute.stanford.edu/encyclopedia /national-council-negro-women-ncnw.

"I've never seen a more immoveable force . . .": Jeanne Theoharis, A More Beautiful and Terrible History: The Uses and Misuses of Civil Rights History (Boston: Beacon Press, 2018), 171.

"became much more aware . . .": Bettye Collier-Thomas and V. P. Franklin, eds., Sisters in the Struggle: African American Women in the Civil Rights–Black Power Movement (New York: NYU Press, 2001), 89.

"sick and tired of being sick and tired": Maegan Parker Brooks and Davis W. Houck, eds., The Speeches of Fannie Lou Hamer: To Tell It Like It Is (Jackson, Miss.: University Press of Mississippi, 2011), 62.

"I didn't know anything . . . we could register and vote": Brooks and Houck, The Speeches of Fannie Lou Hamer, 23.

"You'll have to go down and withdraw . . .": Brooks and Houck, The Speeches of Fannie Lou Hamer, 26.

"the lady who sings the hymns": Charles Marsh, God's Long Summer: Stories of Faith and Civil Rights (Princeton, N.J.: Princeton University Press, 1997), 17.

"walked over, took my dress . . .": Danielle L. McGuire, At the Dark End of the Street: Black Women, Rape, and Resistance—a New History of the Civil Rights Movement from Rosa Parks to the Rise of Black Power (New York: Alfred A. Knopf, 2010), 194.

"unshaven and unwanted trash": Yasuhiro Katagiri, Black Freedom, White Resistance, and Red Menace: Civil Rights and Anticommunism in the Jim Crow South (Baton Rouge, La.: Louisiana State University Press, 2014), 231.

"I'm showing the people . . .": Jerry DeMuth, "Fannie Lou Hamer: Tired of Being Sick and Tired," The Nation, June 1, 1964, https://www.thenation.com/article/fannie-lou-hamer-tired-being-sick-and-tired/.

"deep, powerful voice . . . shakes the air": DeMuth, The Nation.

"All of this is on account . . . human beings, in America?": Todd J. Moye, Let the People Decide: Black Freedom and White Resistance Movements in Sunflower County, Mississippi, 1945–1986 (Chapel Hill, N.C.: University of North Carolina Press, 2004), 138.

"Do you mean to tell me . . .": Lawrence O'Donnell Jr., Playing with Fire: The 1968 Election and the Transformation of American Politics (New York: Penguin Press, 2017), 330.

"Then they charged. They came . . .": Jane Ridley, "103-year-old activist: I was almost killed fighting for freedom," New York Post, December 1, 2014, https://nypost.com/2014/12/01/103-year-old-activist-i-was-almost-killed-fighting-for-freedom/.

"it could have killed me. . . fear that is in our people": C. G. Freightman, "Amelia Boynton Robinson, 104: Fought for voting rights," Atlanta Journal-Constitution, August 26, 2015, https://www.ajc.com/news /breaking-news/amelia-boynton-robinson-104-fought-for-voting-rights/liraycNGE5sf7gc6D2JkYM/.

"There is no cause for pride . . . justice, to serve man": Lyndon B. Johnson, "President Johnson's Special Message to the Congress: The American Progress," LBJ Presidential Library, March 15, 1965, http://www.lbjlibrary.org /lyndon-baines-johnson/speeches-films/president-johnsons-special-message-to-the-congress-the-american-promise.

"eliminate illegal barriers to the right to vote": Johnson, "President Johnson's Special Message to the Congress."

"There is no constitutional issue . . . struggle for human rights": Johnson, "President Johnson's Special Message to the Congress."

"Today there are no poll taxes . . .": Editorial Board, "The Voting Rights Act at 50," The New York Times, August 5, 2015, https://www.nytimes.com/2015/08/05/opinion/the-voting-rights-act-at-50.html.

Epilogue: Continuing to Climb

"heart of the Voting Rights Act": Kristen Clarke and Ezra Rosenberg, "Trump administration has Voting Rights Act on life support," CNN, August 6, 2018, https://www.cnn.com/2018/08/06/opinions/voting-rights-act-anniversary-long-way -to-go-clarke-rosenberg-opinion/index.html.

"decades-old data and eradicated practices . . . no longer such a disparity": Vann R. Newkirk II, "How *Shelby County v. Holder* Broke America," *The Atlantic*, July 10, 2018, theatlantic.com/politics/archive/2018/07/how-shelby-county-broke-america/564707/.

"The formula captures States . . .": Newkirk, "How *Shelby County v. Holder* Broke America."

"throwing out preclearance when . . .": Newkirk, "How *Shelby County v. Holder* Broke America."

"continue to suffer significant . . .": United States Commission on Civil Rights, "An Assessment of Minority Voting Rights Access in the United States," September 12, 2018, https://www.usccr.gov/press/2018/09-12-18-PR.pdf.

"Voter suppression isn't only . . .": Sarah Ruiz-Grossman and Sam Levine, "Georgia Candidate Brian Kemp Claims Voter Suppression Is a 'Farce,' Blames Obama," *Huffington Post*, October 23, 2018, https://www.huffpost.com/entry/stacey-abrams-brian-kemp-governor-debate-georgia_n_5bcfd603e4b055bc94860d4d.

"Voter suppression happens in every . . . people have to respond": Emma Newburger, "Stacey Abrams, after narrow election loss, vows to fight for voter rights," CNBC, March 8, 2019, https://www.cnbc.com/2019/03/08/stacey-abrams-vows-to-fight-for -voter-rights-with-fight-fair-action.html.

Acknowledgments

Writing is a solitary endeavor. You sit down, usually alone, research, write, and revise—spending more time in your mind than out of it. Nobody is really able to see is all the people standing in the gap for you, supporting you, training you, preparing you—me—for this moment. I am in gratitude to them always, and especially right now.

Thank you to the women, past, present, and future, who paved the way for me to be a writer who gets to tell Black women's history. Zora Neale Hurston. Alice Walker. Ida B. Wells-Barnett. Maya Angelou. Pearl Cleage. Ntozake Shange. Toni Morrison. Had I not read your words, I would never have known this were possible. I am indebted to you, always.

My greatest teachers prepared me for this moment. I could not be me without you. Dr. Keonte Coleman, thank you for teaching me the value of crossing t's and dotting i's. There are no shortcuts. Dr. Yvonne Welbon, thank you for holding me accountable—to the work and to myself. You were the very first person to tell me I was a feminist. I'm sorry I didn't believe you, but now I live in that purpose every single day. Professor Tamara Jeffries, thank you for teaching me humility and grace. For telling me I was a writer. For turning me into an editor. For your endless patience. There is no greater honor than being your forever student. Professor Penny Speas, you introduced me to Alice Walker. It changed the course of my life. Thank you.

Sarah Phair, my incredible agent, took a chance on a writer and editor who didn't even know she could write a book. She still gets in the trenches with me and for that I'm eternally grateful. Venturing into the world of middle-grade nonfiction was never on my radar until Sheila Keenan told me I could write this book and then championed me through a long, arduous process with many health complications and many missed deadlines. Thank you for believing in me, believing in this process, and believing that this story was worth telling. Jenny Bak, thank you for shepherding this project over the finish line. Kate Renner, the artist who designed this cover, captured its essence in a way I am forever grateful for, and Viking's entire copyediting squad made this book dazzle. From editor to editor, I thank you.

My friends put up with me when I was unreachable. They loved me despite my absences. Christian, Antasha, Erica, Candyce, and Briana, I love y'all forever—and then another day. My family put up with me too. They let me miss birthdays and family dinners without holding a single grudge. That's a sustaining love. Aunt Tracey, Bria, Uncle Daryl, and Aunt Dorothy, I owe you—a whole lot. I love you forever. Grandma, you are the fiercest woman to ever grace the Earth. You've taught me the value of independence, the beauty in being able to dictate my own course. I even inherited your love of reading. There are not enough words in the English language to thank you. I love you. I hope I've made you proud. Shameika, my very best friend and the person who sharpens me mentally, emotionally, and creatively, thank you for holding me down, being in the trenches with me, and reminding me, every day, that I could do this.

My parents and my brother—words can't describe how grateful I am for you. When I thought I would quit on this project and many others, you held me up, let me cry, and championed me across the finish line. I do it all for us. All of it. Every late night, every night without sleep, every night that I cried and felt like giving up is for us. For our family. For our family's legacy. And lastly, to my nieces, Melonie and Maddison, I wrote this book for you. For you to know your history—our history. I hope you're proud of auntie because I am surely proud of you.

Photo Credits

Page 9: Library of Congress Prints and Photographs Division [LC-USZ62-39380]

Page 10: Library Company of Philadelphia

Page 13: Library of Congress [LC-USZ62-118946]

Page 14: Library of Congress Prints and Photographs Division [LC-USZ62-44563]

Page 15: Bryan Arnold (@nanowhiskers)

Page 16: Library of Congress, Prints & Photographs Division, Visual Materials from the Rosa Parks Papers, [LC-DIG-ppmsca-38464]

Page 18: Open Road Media

Page 19: General Negative Collection, North Carolina State Archives, Raleigh, NC

Page 20: Library of Congress Prints and Photographs Division [LC-DIG-ppmsca-54230]

Page 23: Library of Congress Manuscript Division, Sojourner Truth Collection (MMC) [LC-USZ62-119343]

Page 33: Kenneth C. Zirkel

Page 33: *The New York Herald*. [volume] (New York [N.Y.]), 30 July, 1848. Chronicling America: Historic American Newspapers. Lib. of Congress.

Page 34: Elizabeth Cady Stanton Papers, Manuscript Division, Library of Congress (009.00.00)

Page 36: Library and Archives Canada/Mary Ann Shadd Cary collection/c029977

Page 38: National Portrait Gallery, Smithsonian Institution

Page 42: Library of Congress Prints and Photographs Division [LC-USZ61-791]

Page 43: Library of Congress Prints and Photographs Division [LC-USZ62-7816]

Page 45: New York State Library, Manuscripts and Special Collections, BRO0119+

Page 47: Library of Congress Prints and Photographs Division [LC-DIG-ppmsca-34808]

Page 48: Library of Congress Prints and Photographs Division [LC-USZ62-60909]

Page 50: Library of Congress Prints and Photographs Division [LC-DIG-bellcm-15413]

Page 53: Library of Congress Prints and Photographs Division [LC-DIG-ppmsca-37947]

Page 57: Mary Garrity

Page 61: Library of Congress Prints and Photographs Division [LC-USZ61-790]

Page 64—65: Library of Congress Prints and Photographs Division [LC-USZ62-54722]

Page 68: Josephine St. Pierre Ruffin. (2011). In Massachusetts Hall of Black Achievement. Item 32.

Page 69: Terrell, Mary Church. Mary Church Terrell Papers: Miscellany, -1954; Printed matter; Woman's Era; 1896. 1896.
          Manuscript/Mixed Material. Library of Congress.

Page 71: National Federation of Afro-American Women. Historical Records of Conventions of 1895—96 of the Colored Women of America.

Page 78: *New-York Tribune*. [volume] (New York [N.Y.]), 01 March 1913. Chronicling America: Historic American Newspapers. Lib. of Congress.

Page 79: Library of Congress Prints and Photographs Division [LC-USZ62-51555]

Page 81: Library of Congress Prints and Photographs Division [LC-DIG-ds-13272]

Page 83: Schomburg Center for Research in Black Culture, Jean Blackwell Hutson Research and Reference Division, The New York Public Library.

Page 87: State Archives of Florida, Florida Memory [N041432]

Page 89: Library of Congress Prints and Photographs Division [LC-DIG-ppmsca-09705]

Page 95: Wells, Ida B. Papers, [Box 10, Folder 1, Photo 6], Special Collections Research Center, University of Chicago Library

Page 96: Library of Congress Prints and Photographs Division [LC-DIG-ppmsca-50312]

Page 98: *Chicago Sunday Tribune* (June 22, 1913), Part 7/Special Features, p. 3. The Janet A. Ginsburg Chicago Tribune Image Collection

Page 101: Library of Congress Prints and Photographs Division [LC-DIG-hec-06766]

Page 102: Library of Congress Prints and Photographs Division [LC-DIG-ppmsca-12512]

Page 104—105: Schomburg Center for Research in Black Culture, Jean Blackwell Hutson Research and Reference Division,
            The New York Public Library.

Page 108: *Chicago Sunday Tribune* (March 5, 1913), p. 5.

Page 111: Library of Congress [LC-USZ62-31799]

Pages 114—115: Missouri Historical Society [N23827]

Page 122: Still Picture Records Section, Special Media Archives Services Division, National Archives Catalog [533032]

Page 124: Special Collections Research Center, University of Chicago Library

Page 127: Still Picture Records Section, Special Media Archives Services Division, National Archives Catalog [535812]

Page 129: Still Picture Records Section, Special Media Archives Services Division, National Archives Catalog [196283]

Page 130: Library of Congress Prints and Photographs Division [LC-DIG-ppmsc-01267]

Page 132: Courtesy Danny Lyon

Page 137: Ianbailey1983. Wikimedia Commons.

Page 140—141: Lyndon Baines Johnson Library and Museum [A1030-17a]

Page 142: Library of Congress Prints and Photographs Division [LC-DIG-ppmsca-55939]

Page 143: Courtesy Michael Fleshman/Flickr

Page 147: Official White House Photo by Pete Souza

Page 148: Official White House Photo by Pete Souza

Index

Note: Page numbers in *italics* refer to illustrations.

VIKING
An imprint of Penguin Random House LLC, New York

First published in the United States of America by Viking,
an imprint of Penguin Random House LLC, 2020

Visit us online at penguinrandomhouse.com

LIBRARY OF CONGRESS CATALOGING-IN-PUBLICATION DATA IS AVAILABLE
ISBN 9780451481542

Printed in the United States of America

Set in Sabon MT Std   Book design by Kate Renner

10   9   8   7   6   5   4   3   2   1